wiener staatsoper

348 complete relays

discography

compiled by

john hunt

Wiener Staatsoper
348 Complete Relays

John Hunt

© John Hunt 2017

ISBN 978-1-901395-32-7

Travis & Emery Music Bookshop
17 Cecil Court
London
WC2N 4EZ
United Kingdom.
Tel. (+44) (0) 20 7240 2129.
newpublications@travis-and-emery.com

CONTENTS

Introduction/*page 5*

part one/**1937-1944**/*page 9*

part two/**1947-1955**/*page 17*

part three/**1955-2015**/*page 23*

part four/**unpublished 1941-2010**/*page 139*

part five/**index of operas**/*page 147*

part six/**index of conductors**/*page 171*

part seven/**a personal collection**/*page 193*

WIENER STAATSOPER: 348 COMPLETE RELAYS
Introduction

The day-to-day activity of Europe's, if not the world's, foremost opera institution has not previously been surveyed in the form of a discography. A large number of short extracts recorded from the stage of the *Wiener Staatsoper* survive from as early as 1933, thanks to the efforts of sound engineer Hermann May, who was given authority by *Operndirektor* Clemens Krauss to document live performances on wax/decelith discs (an extensive selection of these was published on CD by the Koch label in the 1990s).

My concern in this volume, however, is to review the far more important tranche of opera recordings which survive in their complete form. The commercial publication of such documents is a comparatively recent development, and many of course remain unauthorised - this does not mean that they should escape scrutiny.

The corpus of these recorded performances stretches from 1937 until the end of 2015, and can be divided into three distinct sections. The first section covers the years of the Third Reich, a period in which the best of what was happening in the Austrian capital was also on show at the Salzburg Festival: the first three items are in fact Salzburg performances. After the Second War the *Wiener Philharmoniker* continued to provide the backbone of the Salzburg Festival, but the Festival's output began to take on its own identity (although some individual productions were still shared).

introduction/continued

The second of the discographiy's sectiona is devoted to that remarkable period of exile prior to the reconstruction of the war-damaged *Staatsoper* building. Following this, the third (and main) section documents the live occasions captured on tape or radio broadcast since the house's reopening in 1955. The performances in all three sections involve Chorus and Orchesra of the *Wiener Staatsoper,* and the participating singers are listed for each performance. A fourth section then goes on to supplement the main discography by listing further performances known to be in circulation but not actually published (this section may not be complete).

Fifth and Sixth sections index the Repertoire and its Conductors respectively. I would describe that repertoire as proudly conservative, and bearing a remarkable resemblance to the one set down by Richard Strauss in a 1945 letter to his disciple Karl Böhm: it would embrace a handful of pre-classical operas, the Mozart canon from *Entführung* to *Zauberflöte,* selected pieces by Beethoven (*Fidelio*), Weber, Berlioz, Gounod and Bizet, then Verdi and Wagner (from *Rienzi* to *Parsifal)* and, of course, most of Richard Strauss. Recent decades have seen greater attention being paid to French and early Italian repertoire; and even the occasional nod in the direction of the contemporary.

7
introduction/concluded

The conductor section highlights what I consider to be the most important component of the operatic experience, and that is the musical director: you will see that there is scarcely a practitioner of significance who has not conducted at the *Wiener Staatsoper*, not just from the ranks of the star conductor but also the reliable *Kapellmeister* with his special understanding of a singer's needs.

Finally a Seventh section, not directly connected to the discography itself, chronicles the evenings which I have personally experienced on my visits to the *Wiener Staatsoper* over a fifty-year span. The old repertory system was still operating when I first visited in 1965 (despite Herbert von Karajan's attempts to modify it), and has only slightly been watered down in the intervening half century: previously one could experience up to six different operas in as many consecutive days, now perhaps only three or four at most.

My concern has not been the numerous prestigious opera recordings undertaken by major record companies in the era of the long-playing record: these employed the *Staatsoper* Orchestra in its concert capacity (*Wiener Philharmoniker*), and even whein claiming to be based on live performance, were often edited into a montage from several different dates
This is a situation which has changed again in recent decades, when economic forces have started to dictate that studio-based opera recordings are rarely feasible.

John Hunt   2016

PART ONE: VIENNA, SALZBURG AND DEN HAAG 1937-1944

001/30 july 1937/salzburg altes festspielhaus
mozart die zauberflöte/conductor arturo toscanini
lp: toscanini society ATS 1025-1027/mrf records MRF 71/
estro armonico EA 056/cetra LO 44
cd: melodram MEL 37040/grammofono AB 78017-78025/
AB 78528-78529/40s label FTO 321-322/naxos 811.0828-0829

Jarmila novotna/julie osvath/dora komarek/helge rosvaenge/alexander kipnis/willi domgraf-fassbaender/william wernigk/alfred jerger/richard sallaba/hilde konetzni/stefania fratnikova/kerstin thorborg/kurt pech/albert feuhl/fritz mascha/anton dermota/carl bissuti

002/2 august 1937/salzburg altes festspielhaus
mozart don giovanni/conductor bruno walter
lp: unique opera recordings UORC 134/discocorp BWS 802/
melodram MEL 716
cd: radio years RY 83-85/eklipse EKRCD 43/legato LCD 114/
omega opera archive OOA 481/opera lovers 193701

ezio pinza/virgilio lazzari/dino borgioli/elisabeth rethberg/luise helletsgruber/margit bokor/herbert alsen/karl ettl

003/5 august 1937/salzburg altes festspielhaus
wagner die meistersinger von nürnberg/conductor
arturo toscanini
lp: toscanini society ATS 1062-1066/mrf records MRF 16/
accent ACC 150040/melodram MEL 012
cd: melodram MEL 47041/eklipse EKRCD 54/grammofono
AB 78703-78706/AB 78017-78025/andante/
immortal performances (canada)

hans hermann nissen/herbert alsen/henk noort/richard sallaba/
maria reining/kerstin thorborg/viktor madin/georg maikl/rolf
telasco/hermann wiedemann/anton dermota/eduard fritsch/
hermann gallos/alfred muzzarelli/carl bissuti/karl ettl

004/11 august 1937/salzburg altes festspielhaus
mozart le nozze di figaro/conductor bruno walter
lp: unique opera recordings UORC 256/discocorp BWS 801
cd: eklipse EKRCD 43/arkadia 50004/istituto discografico
italiano IDIS 6376-6377/andante 3981

aulikki rautawaara/ester rethy/jarmila novotna/dora komarek/
angelica krawtschenko/mariano stabile/ezio pinza/william
wernigk/virgilio lazzari

005/23 august 1937/salzburg altes festspielhaus
verdi falstaff/conductor arturo toscanini
lp: toscanini society ATS 1067-1069/penzance PR 37/morgan
MOR 3701/cetra LO 46
cd: di stefano GDS 21014/minerva MNA 36-37/arkadia CD 625/
CDHP 625/40s label FTS 321-322/grammofono AB 78707-78708/
AB 78017-78025/bongiovanni 1137-1138/andante 3080/
opera lovers 193601

mariano stabile/piero biasini/dino borgioli/franca somigli/augusta
oltrabella/mita vasari/angelica cravcenco/alfredo tedeschi/giuseppe nessi

006/10 june 1939/wiener staatsoper
strauss friedenstag/conductor clemens krauss
cd: koch 3-1465-2

hans hotter/viorica ursuleac/herbert alsen/Josef witt/hermann wiedemann/
carl bissuti/nikolaus zec/anton dermota/hermann gallos/georg monthy/
franz schramm/erich majkut/raimund loibnegger/karl kamann/
willy franter/viktor madin/mela bugarinovic
performance of the opera is preceded by strauss fanfare der stadt wien

007/15 march 1940/guest performance in den haag gebouw voor kunsten en wetenschappen
mozart le nozze di figaro/conductor hans knappertsbusch/
sung in german
cd: tahra TAH 573-574

alfred poell/paul schöffler/maria reining/elisabeth rutgers/dora komarek/olga levko-antosch/maria schober/franz normann/ anton arnold/viktor madin/hermann gallos

008/2 august 1941/salzburg altes festspielhaus
mozart die zauberflöte/conductor karl böhm
cd: myto MCD 981010

maria reining/lea piltti/dora komarek/peter anders/alfred poell/ ludwig weber/karl wessely/william wernigk/hilde konetzni/dora with/elena nikolaidi/erika pirschl/elfriede trötschel/anny schneller/willy franter/franz normann

009/5 august 1942/salzburg altes festspielhaus
mozart le nozze di figaro/conductor clemens krauss/
sung in german
cd: preiser 90203/grammofono AB 78665-78667

helena braun/Irma beilke/gerda sommerschuh/res fischer/ liane timm/hans hotter/erich kunz/Josef witt/gustav neidlinger/ franz normann/william wernigk

010/9 august 1942/salzburg altes festspielhaus
strauss arabella/conductor clemens krauss
cd: myto MCD 92154/983.HO19/cantus classics 500367/
omega opera archive OOA 891

viorica ursuleac/trude eipperle/hans reinmar/theo herrmann/luise willer/else böttcher/ruth michaelis/horst taubmann/franz klarwein/ odo ruepp/alfred poell/william wernigk/emanuel haller/viktor maiwald/ emil graf/frieda haller/johann hahn/franz polcar/franz kolin/alfred muzzarelli/ferdinand oesterer

011/31 may-1 june 1943/reichsrundfunk recording without audience in wiener musikvereinssaal
verdi macbeth/conductor karl böhm/*sung in german*
lp: urania URLP 220/acanta DE 23277-23278
cd: preiser 90175/cantus classics 500098/
omega opera archive OOA 295

mathieu ahlersmayer/elisabeth höngen/else böttcher/herbert alsen/ Josef witt/willy franter/viktor madin/karl ettl/hermann baier

012/7-9 february 1944/reichsrundfunk recording without audience in wiener konzerthaus
beethoven fidelio/conductor karl böhm
lp: vox PL 7793/acanta DE 23116-23117
cd: preiser 90195/grammofono AB 78807-78809/cantus classics 500068/andante 3090

hilde konetzni/irmgard seefried/torsten ralf/peter klein/paul schöffler/tomislav neralic/herbert alsen/hermann gallos/hans schweiger

013/15-17 may 1944/reichsrundfunk recording without audience in wiener musikvereinssaal
strauss daphne/conductor karl böhm
cd: preiser 90237/omega opera archive OOA 4553

maria reining/melanie frutschnigg/emmy loose/maria schober/anton dermota/karl friedrich/richard sallaba/georg monthy/hans schweiger/hermann baier

014/11 june 1944/wiener staatsoper
strauss ariadne auf naxos/conductor karl böhm
lp: deutsche grammophon LPM 18550-18852/discocorp IGI 378/acanta DE 23309-23310
cd: preiser 90217/koch 3-1473-2/arlecchino ARLA 14-16

maria reining/irmgard seefried/alda noni/max lorenz/paul schöffler/josef witt/alfred muzzarelli/friedrich jelinek/hermann baier/hans schweiger/emmy loose/melanie frutschnigg/elisabeth rutgers/erich kunz/richard sallaba/marjan rus/peter klein

015/30 september-3 october 1944/reichsrundfunk recording without audience in wiener staatsoper
verdi otello/conductor karl böhm/*sung in german*
cd: myto MCD 92260/preiser 90230/cantus classics 500096/ house of opera CDBB 76/audio encyclopedia AE 208

hilde konetzni/elena nikolaidi/torsten ralf/paul schöffler/Josef witt/ peter klein/viktor madin/tomislav neralic

016/28 november-5 december 1944/reichsrundfunk recording without audience in wiener musikvereinssaal
wagner die meistersinger von nürnberg/conductor karl böhm
cd: preiser 90234/arkadia 78061/cantus classics 500143

irmgard seefried/else schürhoff/august seider/peter klein/paul schöffler/herbert alsen/erich kunz/fritz krenn/georg maikl/ william wernigk/alfred muzzarelli/Josef witt/alfred jerger/ marjan rus/viktor madin

PART TWO: STAATSOPER IN EXILE/THEATER AN DER WIEN AND LONDON 1947-1955

017/24 september 1947/guest performance in london
royal opera house
beethoven fidelio/conductor clemens krauss
cd: istituto discografico italiano IDIS 6379-6380

hilde konetzni/elisabeth schwarzkopf/karl friedrich/peter klein/ludwig weber/paul schöffler/hermann gallos/hans schweiger

018/30 september 1947/guest performance in london
royal opera house
strauss salome/conductor clemens krauss
cd: legato LCD 211/gebhardt JGCD 0011-0012/
opera lovers 194701

maria cebotari/elisabeth höngen/dagmar herrmann/marko rothmüller/julius patzak/karl friedrich/peter klein/william wernigk/maximilian willimsky/erwin nowaro/ljubomir pantscheff/ludwig weber/hans schweiger/wilhelm felden/hans braun/alfred muzzarelli/erich majkut

019/28 march 1953/staatsoper im theater an der wien
wagner der fliegende holländer/conductor rudolf moralt
cd: golden melodram GM 10081

christel goltz/rosette anday/max lorenz/otto edelmann/gottlob frick/anton dermota

020/12 october 1953/staatsoper im theater an der wien
beethoven fidelio/conductor wilhelm furtwängler
lp: replica RPL 2439-2441/cetra FE 8-10
cd: cetra CDC 12/priceless D 20902/rodolphe RPC 32494/ virtuoso 269 7272/andante 3090/premiere 1160/archipel ARPCD 0181/Japanese furtwängler centre WFHC 028-029/ chibas restorations 1137-1139

martha mödl/sena jurinac/wolfgang windgassen/rudolf schock/ gottlob frick/otto edelmann/alfred poell/hermann gallos/ franz bierbach

021/30 march 1954/staatsoper im theater an der wien
strauss intermezzo/conductor rudolf moralt
cd: omega opera archive OOA 538

hilde zadek/anny felbermayer/dorothea frass/alfred poell/rudolf christ/hugo meyer-welfing/franz bierbach/oskar czerwenka/ adolf vogel/herbert alsen

022/15 september 1954/guest performance in london royal festival hall
mozart don giovanni/conductor karl böhm
cd: archipel ARPCD 0234/premiere 1165/omega opera archive OOA 691/opera lovers 195402

elisabeth grümmer/sena jurinac/emmy loose/george london/ leopold simoneau/erich kunz/herald pröglhöf/ludwig weber

023/4 october 1954/staatsoper im theater an der wien
wagner die meistersinger von nürnberg/conductor karl böhm
cd: omega opera archive OOA 392

Irmgard seefried/elisabeth höngen/set svanholm/murray dickie/ paul schöffler/herbert alsen/erich kunz/harald pröglhöf/hans schweiger/hugo meyer-welfing/fritz krenn/erich majkut/ hermann gallos/erwin nowaro/franz bierbach/alfred muzzarelli

024/26 february 1955/staatsoper im theater an der wien
giordano andrea chenier/conductor rudolf moralt/
sung in german
cd: relief 1919/omega opera archive OOA 242/
opera depot OD 10161

hilde zadek/elisabeth höngen/marta rohs/helge rosvaenge/theo bayle/ljubomir pantscheff/herald pröglhöf/erich majkut/hans schweiger/fritz sperlbauer/franz bierbach/wilhelm leninger/ frederick guthrie/adolf vogel

025/17 june 1955/staatsoper im theater an der wien
tchaikovsky evgeny onegin/conductor berislav klobucar/
sung in german
cd: myto MCD 005233/great opera performances
GOP 66342/opera depot OD 10049

leonie rysanek/mira kalin/polly batic/hilde rössel-majdan/ george london/anton dermota/gottlob frick/ljubomir pantscheff/peter klein

PART THREE: WIENER STAATSOPER, MOSCOW AND TOKYO 1955-2015

026/5 november 1955/wiener staatsoper
beethoven fidelio/conductor karl böhm
lp: melodram MEL 008
cd: memoria CMM 2/movimento musica 051.024/
walhall WLCD 0157/orfeo C813 102I

martha mödl/irmgard seefried/anton dermota/waldemar kmentt/
paul schöffler/karl kamann/ludwig weber/karl terkal/alfred jerger

027/6 november 1955/wiener staatsoper
mozart don giovanni/conductor karl böhm/
sung in german
cd: rca/bmg 74321 577372/omega opera archive OOA 862

sena jurinac/lisa della casa/irmgard seefried/george london/
anton dermota/erich kunz/ludwig weber/walter berry

028/9 november 1955/wiener staatsoper
strauss die frau ohne schatten/conductor karl böhm
cd: orfeo C668 053D/premiere 2057

leonie rysanek/christel goltz/elisabeth höngen/hans hopf/
ludwig weber/kurt böhme/judith hellwig/emmy loose/hilde
rössel-majdan/karl terkal/herald pröglhöf/oskar czerwenka/
murray dickie

029/11 november 1955/wiener staatsoper
verdi aida/conductor rafael kubelik/*sung in german*
lp: legendary recordings LR 145
cd: legato SRO 572/myto MCD 023267/premiere 1507/
walhall WLCD 0114/omega opera archive OOA 766/
opera depot OD 10251

leonie rysanek/jean madeira/hans hopf/george london/gottlob
frick/oskar czerwenka/erich majkut/anny felbermayer

030/14 november 1955/wiener staatsoper
wagner die meistersinger von nürnberg/conductor fritz reiner
cd: melodram CDM 47083/orfeo C667 054/cantus classics 500192/walhall WLCD 0163/omega opera archive 4140/ opera lovers 195501

irmgard seefried/rosette anday/hans beirer/murray dickie/paul schöffler/gottlob frick/erich kunz/karl terkal/eberhard waechter/ hans braun/erich majkut/fritz sperlbauer/william wernigk/harald pröglhöf/adolf vogel/ljubomir pantscheff/frederick guthrie

031/16 november 1955/wiener staatsoper
strauss der rosenkavalier/conductor hans knappertsbusch
lp: hans-knappertsbusch-gesellschaft (japan) HK 1012-1015
cd: golden melodram GM 30025/rca-bmg 74321 694312/ 74321 694282

maria reining/sena jurinac/hilde güden/kurt böhme/alfred poell/ judith hellwig/hilde rössel-majdan/karl terkal/lazslo szemere/ harald pröglhöf/william wernigk/ljubomir pantscheff/adolf vogel/ berta seidl/erich majkut/fritz sperlbauer

032/25 november 1955/wiener staatsoper
berg wozzeck/conductor karl böhm
cd: andante 3060/opera lovers 195501

christel goltz/polly batic/walter berry/max lorenz/murray dickie/
peter klein/karl dönch/marjan rus/harald pröglhöfwilliam wernigk

033/12 february 1956/wiener staatsoper
wagner tristan und isolde/conductor andre cluytens
cd: walhall WLCD 0235

gertrude grob-prandl/georgine von milinkovic/rudolf lustig/
toni blankenheim/kurt böhme/hans braun/harald pröglhöf/
hugo meyer-welfing/julius patzak

034/6 march 1956/wiener staatsoper
puccini turandot/conductor mario rossi/*sung in german*
cd: walhall WLCD 0160

gertrude grob-prandl/lotte rysanek/karl terkal/Josef greindl/
harald pröglhöf/eberhard waechter/peter klein/murray dickie

035/2 april 1957/wiener staatsoper
wagner die walküre/conductor herbert von karajan
cd: lyric distribution 447/omega opera archive OOA 610/
private edition vienna

birgit nilsson/leonie rysanek/jean madeira/ludwig suthaus/hans hotter/gottlob frick/ljuba welitsch/gerda scheyrer/judith hellwig/ christa ludwig/margareta sjoestedt/marta rohs/rosette anday/ hilde rössel-majdan/lotte rysanek/dorothea frass

036/25 october 1959/wiener staatsoper
rossini la cenerentola/conductor alberto erede/
sung in german
cd: omega opera archive 1280

christa ludwig/emmy loose/dagmar hermann/waldemar kmentt/ walter berry/karl dönch/ludwig welter

037/6 february 1960/wiener staatsoper
borodin prince igor/conductor lovro von matacic/
sung in german
cd: gala GL 100 615/premiere 890
gala edition was incorrectly dated 6 february 1969

hilde zadek/ira malaniuk/eberhard waechter/giuseppe zampieri/ hans hotter/gottlob frick/erich majkut/karl dönch/peter klein/ ilona steingruber/margareta sjoestedt

038/9 march 1960/wiener staatsoper
pizzetti assassino nelle cattedrale/conductor herbert von karajan/
sung in german
cd: deutsche grammophon 457 6712/omega opera
archive 1424/house of opera HO 2740

hans hotter/hilde zaek/christa ludwig/anton dermota/kurt equiluz/
claude heater/edmond hurshell/gerhard stolze/paul schöffler/
walter berry/walter kreppel

039/16 may 1960/wiener staatsoper
strauss capriccio/conductor karl böhm
cd: omega opera archive OOA 566/private edition vienna

elisabeth schwarzkopf/christel goltz/erika köth/anton dermota/
hermann uhde/walter berry/paul schöffler/peter klein/giuseppe
zampieri/alois pernerstorfer/ljubomir pantscheff/fritz sperlbauer/
harald pröglhöf/franz bierbach/erich majkut/karl weber/georg pichler

040/26 june 1960/wiener staatsoper
giordano andrea chenier/conductor lovro von matacic
lp: morgan MOR 6003/mrf records MRF 60
cd: cetra CDE 1017/fabbri OP 10/golden melodram GM 50021/
orfeo C682 062/opera depot 10005/opera lovers 196003/
omega opera archive OOA 248

renata tebaldi/franco corelli/ettore bastianini/elisabeth höngen/
margareta sjoestedt/edmond hurshell/alois pernerstorfer/renato
ercolani/kostas paskalis/fritz sperlbauer/endre koreh/harald
pröglhöf/franz bierbach/ludwig welter/hilde konetzni

041/23 september 1960/wiener staatsoper
verdi la forza del destino/conductor dimitri mitropoulos
lp: morgan MOR 6002/melodram MEL 023
cd: di stefano GDS 31022/myto MCD 002228/orfeo C681 062/
gala GL 100 819/omega opera archive OOA 1336

antonietta stella/giulietta simionato/giuseppe di stefano/ettore
bastianini/ludwig welter/annemarie ludwig/walter kreppel/
karl dönch/harald pröglhöf/hugo meyer-welfing/franz bierbach

042/31 october 1960/wiener staatsoper
lortzing der wildschütz/conductor heinz wallberg
cd: orfeo C786 092

irmgard seefried/hilde rössel-majdan/waldemar kmentt/georg völker/
anny felbermayer/renate holm/karl dönch/peter klein/franz bierbach

043/11 november 1960/wiener staatsoper
smetana the bartered bride/conductor berislav klobucar/
sung in german
cd: orfeo C785 092

irmgard seefried/hilde konetzni/rosette anday/liselotte maikl/murray dickie/waldemar kmentt/ludwig welter/oskar czerwenka/hans schweiger

044/27 november 1960/wiener staatsoper
beethoven fidelio/conductor herbert von karajan
cd: golden melodram GM 50053/private edition vienna

aase nordmo-lövberg/wilma lipp/wolfgang windgassen/murray dickie/ walter kreppel/hans hotter/otto wiener/karl terkal/ljubomir pantscheff

045/31 december 1960/wiener staatsoper
johann strauss die fledermaus/conductor herbert von karajan
lp: foyer FO 1031
cd: foyer 3CF-2021/arkadia CDKAR 215/rca-bmg 74321 619492/74321 619532

hilde güden/rita streich/elfriede ott/giuseppe zampieri/eberhard waechter/erich kunz/gerhard stolze/walter berry/peter klein/ josef meinrad/giuseppe di stefano

046/26 january 1961/wiener staatsoper
tchaikovsky evgeny onegin/conductor lovro von matacic/
sung in german
lp: melodram MEL 046
cd: gala GL 100 741

sena jurinac/hilde konetzni/biserka cvejic/hilde rössel-majdan/
dietrich fischer-dieskau/anton dermota/walter kreppel/peter klein

047/25 march 1961/wiener staatsoper
puccini madama butterfly/conductor berislav klobucar
cd: myto MCD 21254/orfeo C767 092

sena jurinac/hilde rössel-majdan/gundula janowitz/ermanno lorenzi/kostas paskalis/peter klein/karl weber/harald pröglhöf/alois pernerstorfer/fritz sperlbauer

048/1 april 1961/wiener staatsoper
wagner parsifal/conductor herbert von karajan
cd: arkadia CDKAR 219/rca-bmg 74321 619502/74321 619352/omega opera archive OOA 2818/
opera d'oro 1169

fritz uhl/christa ludwig/elisabeth höngen/eberhard waechter/hans hotter/tugomir franc/walter berry/liselotte maikl/margareta sjoestedt/gundula janowitz/hilde güden/anneliese rothenberger/gerda scheyrer/hilde rössel-majdan/erich majkut/kurt equiluz/ermanno lorenzi/kostas paskalis

049/22 june 1961/wiener staatsoper
puccini turandot/conductor francesco molinari-pradelli
cd: orfeo C813 102

birgit nilsson/leontyne price/giuseppe di stefano/nicola zaccaria/peter klein/alois pernerstorfer/kostas paskalis/ermanno lorenzi/murray dickie

050/3 october 1961/wiener staatsoper
verdi don carlo/conductor nello santi
cd: omega opera archive OOA 1513/opera depot OD 10148

antonietta stella/giulietta simionato/flaviano labo/eberhard waechter/
walter kreppel/nicola zaccaria/frederick guthrie/kurt equiluz/erich
majkut/karl friedrich/anny felbermayer/elfi hlinak/liselotte maikl

051/8 november 1961/wiener staatsoper
poulenc dialogues des carmelites/conductor berislav klobucar/
sung in german
cd: ponto 1041

emmy loose/elisabeth höngen/hilde zadek/christel goltz/rosette anday/
anneliese rothenberger/margareta sjoestedt/Julia lichtblau/rudolf knoll/
laszlo szemere/alois pernerstorfer/erich majkut/ljubomir pantscheff/
hans schweiger/herald pröglhöf

052/10 december 1961/wiener staatsoper
bizet carmen/conductor herbert von karajan
cd: arkadia CDKAR 201

regina resnik/hilde güden/dimiter usunow/aldp protti/liselotte maikl/
hilde rössel-majdan/ludwig welter/alfred poell/murray dickie/
harald pröglhöf/fritz klos

053/6 january 1962/wiener staatsoper
debussy pelleas et melisande/conductor herbert von karajan
cd: private edition vienna

henri gui/eberhard waechter/hilde güden/elisabeth höngen/adriana martino/nicola zaccaria/alfred poell

054/29 january 1962/wiener staatsoper
puccini tosca/conductor herbert von karajan
cd: arkadia CDKAR 206

floriana cavalli/dimiter usunow/aldo protti/ferruccio mazzoli/karl dönch/erich makjut/harald pröglhöf/ljubomir pantscheff

055/3 february 1962/wiener staatsoper
verdi rigoletto/conductor tullio serafin
cd: omega opera archive 3830

aldo protti/giuseppe zampieri/ruth-margret pütz/giulietta simionato/
rudolf knoll/ljubomir pantscheff/liselotte maikl/siegfried rudolf frese/
kurt equiluz/ferruccio mazzoli/Judith hellwig/laurence dutoit/herald pröglhöf

056/25 may 1962/wiener staatsoper
beethoven fidelio/conductor herbert von karajan
lp: movimento musica 03.014
cd: deutsche grammophon 477 7364

christa ludwig/gundula janowitz/jon vickers/waldemar kmentt/
walter kreppel/eberhard waechter/walter berry/kostas paskalis/ljubomir pantscheff

057/30 may 1962/staatsoper im theater an der wien
mozart die zauberflöte/conductor herbert von karajan
lp: movimento musica 03.015
cd: movimento musica 051.028

wilma lipp/graziella sciutti/ingeborg hallstein/nicolai gedda/erich kunz/
gottlob frick/eberhard waechter/paul kuen/gerda scheyrer/grace
hofmann/hilde rössel-majdan/ermanno lorenzi/kostas paskalis/
frederick guthrie

058/22 june 1962/wiener staatsoper
mozart don giovanni/conductor joseph keilberth
cd: omega opera archive OOA 1611

gerda scheyrer/elisabeth schwarzkopf/graziella sciutti/rudolf jedlicka/
nicolai gedda/walter berry/nicola zaccaria/ljubomir pantscheff

059/8 january 1963/wiener staatsoper
wagner tannhäuser/conductor herbert von karajan
lp: melodram MEL 427
cd: nuova era NE 6307-6309/deutsche grammophon
457 6822/arkadia CDKAR 204/omega opera archive
OOA 833/opera lovers 196301

gre brouwenstijn/christa ludwig/gundula janowitz/hans beirer/eberhard
waechter/waldmar kmentt/ludwig welter/kurt equiluz/tugomir franc

060/1 april 1963/wiener staatsoper
monteverdi l'incoronazione di poppea/conductor
herbert von karajan
cd: deusche grammophon 457 6742/premiere 1637

sena jurinac/margarita lilowa/hilde rössel-majdan/gundula janowitz/
gerhard stolze/otto wiener/carlo cava/olivero miljakovic/gerda
scheyrer/murray dickie/siegfried rudolf frese/ermanno lorenzi

061/27 april 1963/theatre an der wien
strauss intermezzo/conductor joseph keilberth
lp: ed smith EJS 344/melodram MEL 113
cd: orfeo C765 082

hanny steffek/anny felbermayer/judith hellwig/hermann prey/
ferry gruber/alfred poell/waldemar kmentt/oskar czerwenka/
alois perenerstorfer/ludwig welter

062/19 may 1963/wiener staatsoper
berg wozzeck/conductor leopold ludwig
cd: omega opera archive OOA 1697

walter berry/christa ludwig/dagmar hermann/fritz uhl/murray dickie/
gerhard stolze/karl dönch/ludwig welter/harald pröglhöf/erich majkut

063/3 june 1963/wiener staatsoper
verdi aida/conductor lovro von matacic
lp: melodram MEL 410/foyer FO 1036
cd: foyer 2CF-2018/omega opera archive OOA 1361/
house of opera CDWW 938/opera lovers 196302

leontyne price/giulietta simionato/dimiter usunow/ettore bastianini/
walter kreppel/tugomir franc

064/22 june 1963/wiener staatsoper
mozart don giovanni/conductor herbert von karajan
cd: gala GL 100 608/verona 27065-27067/
omega opera archive OOA 824

leontyne price/hilde güden/graziella sciutti/fritz wunderlich/eberhard
waechter/walter berry/walter kreppel/rolando panerai

065/9 november 1963/wiener staatsoper
puccini la boheme/conductor herbert von karajan
lp: melodram MEL 414/movimento musica 02.020
cd: melodram MEL 27007/movimento musica 051.027/
rodolphe RPC 32513/curcio OP 1/arkadia CDMP 477/rca-bmg
74321 577362

mirella freni/hilde güden/gianni raimondi/giuseppe taddei/rolando panerai/ivo vinco/peter klein/siegfried rudolf frese/kurt equiluz

066/7 march 1964/wiener staatsoper
janacek jenufa/conductor jarolslav krombholc/*sung in german*
cd: myto MCD 023066/opera lovers 196401/
opera depot OD 10150

sena jurinac/martha mödl/elisabeth höngen/waldemar kmentt/jean cox/ hans braun/ljubomir pantscheff/hilde konetzni/lucia popp/olivera miljakovic/anny felbermayer/dagmar hermann/annemarie ludwig

067/21 march 1964/wiener staatsoper
strauss capriccio/conductor georges pretre
cd: omega opera archive OOA 1540/orfeo C734 082

lisa della casa/christa ludwig/lucia popp/fritz wunderlich/waldemar kmentt/robert kerns/walter berry/otto wiener/peter klein/alois pernerstorfer

068/8 june 1964/wiener staatsoper/*dress rehearsal performance*
strauss die frau ohne schatten/conductor herbert von karajan
cd: gala GL 100 607/omega opera archive OOA 4493/
opera depot OD 10213

gundula janowitz/gladys kuchta/grace hofmann/jess thomas/otto wiener/walter kreppel/lucia popp/ermanno lorenzi/margarita lilowa/siegfried rudolf frese/ludwig welter/erich majkut

069/11 june 1964/wiener staatsoper
strauss die frau ohne schatten/conductor herbert von karajan
cd: nuova era NE 2288-2290/arkadia CDKAR 207/deutsche grammophon 457 6782/opera lovers 196401

leonie rysanek/christa ludwig/grace hofmann/jess thomas/walter berry/walter kreppel/lucia popp/fritz wunderlich/margarita lilowa/ siegfried rudolf frese/ludwig welter/erich majkut

070/14 june 1964/wiener staatsoper
verdi aida/conductor herbert von karajan
cd: audio encyclopedia AE 103

leontyne price/giulietta simionato/flavio labo/ettore bastianini/nicola zaccaria/ludwig weber/gerda scheyrer/ermanno lorenzi

071/27 october 1964/wiener staatsoper
verdi la traviata/conductor berislav klobucar
cd: melodram CDM 27510

anna moffo/giuseppe zampieri/ettore bastianini/laurence dutoit/ margareta sjoestedt/ermanno lorenzi/hans christian/siegfried rudolf frese/herbert lackner/kurt equiluz/fritz sperlbauer/ hans schweiger

072/29 october 1964/wiener staatsoper
puccini manon lescaut/conductor mario rossi
cd: premiere 1390

antonietta stella/gastone limarilli/kostas paskalis/Ludwig welter/ harald pröglhöf/ermanno lorenzi/margarita sjoestedt/kurt equiluz/ giorgio goretti/herbert lackner/hans christian

41

073/16 december 1964/wiener staatsoper
pfitzner palestrina/conductor robert heger
lp: ed smith EJS 521
cd: myto MCD 92259

fritz wunderlich/sena jurinac/christa ludwig/hilde rössel-majdan/gottlob frick/walter berry/gerhard stolze/walter kreppel/otto wiener/ludwig welter/peter klein/herald pröglhöf/robert kerns/gerhard unger/erich majkut/alois pernerstorfer/hans braun/fritz sperlbauer/kurt equiluz/ ljubomir pantscheff/dagmar hermann/hans christian/herbert lackner/ siegfried rudolf frese/karl terkal/tugomir franc/frederick guthrie/ mimi coertse/lucia popp/gundula janowitz

074/12 february 1965/wiener staatsoper
shostakovich katerina ismailova/conductor jaroslav krombholc/
sung in german
cd: legato SRO 567

ludmilla dvorakova/ruthilde boesch/paul schöffler/karl terkal/peter klein/ hans christian/harald pröglhöf/siegfried rudolf frese/fritz sperlbauer/ giorgio goretti/kurt equiluz/georg schnapka/alois pernserstorfer/ tugomir franc/Judith hellwig/dagmar hermann/ljubomir pantscheff

075/16 may 1965/wiener staatsoper
wagner lohengrin/conductor karl böhm
cd: golden melodram GM 10045/orfeo C862 133
omega opera archive OOA 1372

claire watson/christa ludwig/jess thomas/walter berry/martti talvela/
eberhard waechter/kurt equiluz/fritz sperlbauer/herbert lackner/
ljubomir pantscheff

076/25 november 1965/wiener staatsoper
strauss salome/conductor zdenek kosler
cd: myto MCD 01212/omega opera archive OOA 1581/
premiere 1499

anja silja/astrid varnay/margarita lilowa/gerhard stolze/eberhard
waechter/fritz wunderlich/murray dickie/heinz zednik/kurt equiluz/
karl terkal/herbert lackner/gerd nienstedt/robert kerns/tugomir
franc/ljubomir pantscheff/hans christian/Laurence dutoit

077/16 december 1965/wiener staatsoper
strauss elektra/conductor karl böhm
lp: historical recording enterprises HRE 314
cd: legato SRO 833/rca-bmg 74321 694272/74321 694282/
premiere 331/opera depot OD 10076/orfeo C886 142
private edition vienna

birgit nilsson/leonie rysanek/regina resnik/wolfgang windgassen/
eberhard waechter/frederick guthrie/margareta sjoestedt/margarita
lilowa/gerhard unger/herbert lackner/danica mastilovic/
margarete ast/gundula janowitz/gerda scheyrer

078/2 april 1966/wiener staatsoper
mozart cosi fan tutte/conductor karl böhm/*sung in german*
cd: omega opera archive OOA 1750

hilde güden/christa ludwig/graziella sciutti/waldemar kmentt/
walter berry/karl dönch

079/24 april 1966/wiener staatsoper
bizet carmen/conductor lorin maazel
cd: orfeo C733 082

christa ludwig/Jeanette pilou/james king/eberhard waechter/lucia
popp/margarita lilowa/oskar czerwenka/reid bunger/murray
dickie/erich kunz

080/28 april 1966/wiener staatsoper
rossini il barbiere di siviglia/conductor karl böhm/
sung in german
lp: teatro dischi TD 502-503
cd: myto MCD 91752/house of opera CDBB 533

reri grist/hilde konetzni/fritz wunderlich/erich kunz/eberhard waechter/
erich kunz/oskar czerwenka/reid bunger/klaus ofczarek/siegfried
rudolf frese

081/18 september 1966/wiener staatsoper
verdi il trovatore/conductor argeo quadri
cd: opera depot OD 10246

gwyneth jones/fiorenza cossotto/james mccracken/mario sereni/
ivo vinco/laurence dutoit/siegfried rudolf frese/rudolf zimmer/
kurt equiluz

082/15 december 1966/wiener staatsoper
puccini tosca/conductor andre cluytens
cd: golden melodram GM 50062

sena jurinac/carlo cossutta/hans hotter/erich kunz/hans christian/
erich majkut/herald pröglhöf/helmut reischütz

083/16 december 1966/wiener staatsoper
debussy pelleas et melisande/conductor andre cluytens
cd: omega opera archive 2575

henri gui/Jeannette pilou/grace hoffman/gabriel bacquier/walter kreppel/hilda de groote/hans braun

084/19 may 1967/wiener staatsoper
verdi don carlo/conductor berislav klobucar
cd: house of opera CDBB 629

gwyneth jones/ruth hesse/placido domingo/kostas paskalis/cesare siepi/ hans hotter/tugomir franc/laurence dutoit/heinz zednik/lotte rysanek/ elfi hlinak

085/25 may 1967/wiener staatsoper
verdi don carlo/conductor berislav klobucar
cd: house of opera CDBB 446

gwyneth jones/christa ludwig/placido domingo/kostas paskalis/nicolai ghiaurov/hans hotter/tugomir franc/laurence dutoit/heinz zednik/ lotte rysanek/elfi hlinak

086/28 may 1967/wiener staatsoper
verdi don carlo/conductor berislav klobucar
cd: house of opera CDWW 635/omega opera archive OOA 1332

antonietta stella/grace bumbry/placido domingo/kostas paskalis/nicolai ghiaurov/hans hotter/frederick guthrie/liselotte maikl/heinz zednik/ lotte rysanek/elfi hlinak

087/14 october 1967/wiener staatsoper
puccini tosca/conductor josef krips
cd: myto MCD 054315

sena jurinac/juan oncina/cesare bardelli/hans braun/manfred jungwirth/
mario guggia/harald pröglhöf/helmut reischütz/ljubomir pantecheff/
margarita lilowa

088/20 november 1967/wiener staatsoper
strauss ariadne auf naxos/conductor karl böhm
cd: omega opera archive OOA 1769/lyric distribution 498

leonie rysanek/tatjana troyanos/renate holm/james king/egon Jordan/
paul schöffler/harald pröglhöf/gerhard unger/siegfried rudolf frese/
ljubomir pantecheff/heinz holecek/kurt equiluz/herbert lackner/
murray dickie/lucia popp/margarita lilowa/gerda scheyrer

089/29 november 1967/wiener staatsoper
strauss ariadne auf naxos/conductor karl böhm
cd: melodram CDM 270105

leonie rysanek/tatjana troyanos/Jeanette scovotti/james king/egon
Jordan/paul schöffler/harald pröglhöf/gerhard unger/siegfried
rudolf frese/ljubomir pantscheff/erich kunz/kurt equiluz/herbert
lackner/murray dickie/arleen auger/margarita lilowa/gerda scheyrer

090/13 april 1968/wiener staatsoper
strauss der rosenkavalier/conductor leonard bernstein
cd: omega opera archive OOA 1616

christa ludwig/gwyneth jones/reri grist/walter berry/erich kunz/waldemar kmentt/emmy loose/margarita lilowa/hilde de groote/murray dickie/harald pröglhöf/karl friedrich/ljubomir pantscheff/herbert lackner/kurt equiluz/ karl terkal

091/17 june 1968/wiener staatsoper
verdi don carlo/conductor silvio varviso
cd: legato SRO 850/premiere 129/opera lovers 196801/ house of opera CDBB 641

sena jurinac/fiorenza cossotto/placido domingo/cesare siepi/mario sereni/ivo vinco/laurence dutoit/erich majkut/tugomir franc/ lotte rysanek

092/26 june 1968/wiener staatsoper
gounod faust/conductor ernst märzendorfer
cd: omega opera archive OOA 1751

placido domingo/cesare siepi/wilma lipp/elisabeth höngen/hilde de groote/mario sereni/hans Christian

093/22 september 1968/wiener staatsoper
mozart cosi fan tutte/conductor Josef krips
cd: orfeo C697 072

gundula janowitz/christa ludwig/olivera miljakovic/adolf dallapozza/
eberhard waechter/walter berry

094/16 december 1968/wiener staatsoper
berg lulu/conductor karl böhm
cd: andante 3050/private edition vienna

anja silja/martha mödl/hilde konetzni/rohangiz yachmi/ernst gutstein/
hans hotter/waldemar kmentt/william blankenship/gerd nienstedt/
oskar czerwenka/hans braun/manfred jungwirth/mario guggia/
heinz zednik

095/28 march 1969/wiener staatsoper
verdi simon boccanegra/conductor Josef krips
cd: myto MCD 022259

eberhard waechter/nicolai ghiaurov/gundula janowitz/carlo cossutta/
robert kerns/manfred jungwirth/mario guggia/margareta sjoestedt

096/19 october 1969/wiener staatsoper
smetana dalibor/conductor josef krips
cd: myto MCD 92465/omega opera archive OOA 1285/
opera d'oro 1434/rca-bmg 74321 577352

leonie rysanek/lotte rysanek/ludovic spiess/eberhard waechter/
oskar czerwenka/walter kreppel/adolf dallapozza/tugomir franc

097/3 april 1970/wiener staatsoper
leoncavallo i pagliacci/conductor berislav klobucar
cd: omega opera archive OOA 1753

placido domingo/lotte rysanek/gianpiero mastromei/murray dickie/
vincenzo sardinero/ljubomir pantscheff/fritz sperlbauer

098/18 april 1970/wiener staatsoper
verdi macbeth/conductor karl böhm
lp: hope records HOPE 254/ed rosen ERR 120/
morgan MOR 7001
cd: legato LCD 143/foyer 2CF-2027/opera d'oro 7027/
omega opera archive OOA 1249/opera lovers 197001/
private edition vienna

sherrill milnes/christa ludwig/carlo cossutta/karl ridderbusch/ewald
aichberger/ljubomir pantscheff/siegfried rudolf frese/harald
pröglhöf/gildis flossmann

099/12 may 1970/wiener staatsoper
pfitzner palestrina/conductor hans swarowsky
cd: private edition vienna

anton dermota/hans hotter/walter berry/olivera miljakovic/gertrude jahn/wolfgang windgassen/frederick guthrie/tugomir franc/manfred jungwirth/heinz zednik/harald pröglhöf/robert kerns/gerhard unger/kurt equiluz/alois pernerstorfer/hans braun/fritz sperlbauer/ewald aichberger/ljubomir pantscheff/dagmar hermann/hans christian/hilde rössel-majdan/rita streich/laurence dutoit/judith hellwig/herbert lackner/siegfried rudolf frese/karl terkal

100/3 june 1970/wiener staatsoper
puccini tosca/conductor berislav klobucar
cd: opera depot OD 10216

leonie rysanek/james king/eberhard waechter/hans braun/karl dönch/kurt equiluz/harald pröglhöf/ljubomir pantscheff/helmut reischütz

101/9 june 1970/wiener staatsoper
beethoven fidelio/conductor leonard bernstein
cd: opera depot OD 10175/first classics (japan) FC 104-105

gwyneth jones/lucia popp/james king/adolf dallapozza/franz crass/
walter berry/gerd nienstedt/karl terkal/herbert lackner

102/24 june 1970/wiener staatsoper
wagner tristan und isolde/conductor horst stein
cd: living stage LS 1021-1023

ingrid bjoner/ruth hesse/hans beirer/walter kreppel/otto wiener/
hans braun/ewald aichberger/harald pröglhöf/peter klein

103/13 september 1970/wiener staatsoper
verdi macbeth/conductor berislav klobucar
cd: premiere 1403/opera depot OD 10127

birgit nilsson/kostas paskalis/ion buzea/tugomir franc/ewald aichberger/ljubomir pantscheff/gildis flossmann/hans christian/ siegfried rudolf frese/rudolf zimmer

104/26 september 1970/wiener staatsoper
verdi rigoletto/conductor carlo franci
lp: historical recording enterprises HRE 816
cd: house of opera HO 898

renata scotto/piero cappuccilli/luciano pavarotti/walter kreppel/vera little/gerd nienstedt/ljubomir pantecheff/harald pröglhöf/kurt equiluz/Judith hellwig/laurence dutoit/siegfried rudolf frese

105/25 october 1970/wiener staatsoper
verdi don carlo/conductor horst stein
lp: hope records HOPE 235/legendary recordings LR 163/morgan MOR 7003
cd: legato SRO 514/legendary recordings LR 1028/myto MCD 983189/rodolphe RPC 32653-32655/pantheon PHC 6614-6616/opera d'oro 7034/opera lovers 197001/orfeo C649 053

gundula janowitz/shirley verrett/franco corelli/eberhard waechter/nicolai ghiaurov/martti talvela/edita gruberova/Judith blegen/ewald aichberger/tugomir franc

106/5 december 1970/wiener staatsoper
strauss die ägyptische helena/conductor josef krips
cd: rca-bmg 74321 694292/74321 694282

gwyneth jones/jess thomas/edita gruberova/mimi coertse/peter glossop/
peter schreier/margarita lilowa/ruthilde boesch/margareta sjoestedt/
liselotte maikl/laurence dutoit/anny felbermayer/dagmar hermann

107/30 january 1971/wiener staatsoper
wagner parsifal/conductor charles vanderzand
cd: premiere 1450/omega opera archive OOA 2603/
opera depot OD 10022

rene kollo/grace hofmann/cesare siepi/tugomir franc/robert kerns/alois
pernerstorfer/liselotte maikl/margareta sjoestedt/renate holm/biserka
cvejic/gerda scheyrer/rohangiz yachmi/hilde rössel-majdan/heinz zednik/
ewald aichberger/karl terkal/siegfried rudolf frese

108/14 march 1971/wiener staatsoper
mozart idomeneo/conductor jaroslav krombholc
cd: ponto 1044

lisa della casa/sena jurinac/waldemar kmentt/werner krenn/reid
bunger/manfred jungwirth

109/1 april 1971/wiener staatsoper
verdi un ballo in maschera/conductor berislav klobucar
cd: house of opera CDBB 932

leonie rysanek/olivera miljakovic/vera little/placido domingo/eberhard waechter/herbert lackner/frederick guthrie/hans christian/mario guggia/ewald aichberger

110/11 april 1971/wiener staatsoper
verdi il trovatore/conductor horst stein
cd: house of opera CDBB 673

lotte rysanek/margarita lilowa/placido domingo/gianpiero astromei/ tugomir franc/liselotte maikl/siegfried rudolf frese/mario guggia/ karl kaslavsky

111/1 may 1971/wiener staatsoper
verdi otello/conductor heinz wallberg
cd: house of opera HO 737

hans beirer/Ingrid bjoner/rohangiz yachmi/piero cappuccilli/giuseppe zampieri/tugomir franc/hans christian/mario guggia

112/23 may 1971/wiener staatsoper
von einem der besuch der alten dame/conductor horst stein
lp: amadeo 419 5521
cd: amadeo 419 5522

christa ludwig/emmy loose/hans beirer/eberhard waechter/hans hotter/
manfred jungwirth/heinz zednik/siegfried rudolf frese/alois pernerstorfer

113/2 june 1971/wiener staatsoper
verdi un ballo in maschera/conductor silvio varviso
cd: omega opera archive 6393

leonie rysanek/biserka cvejic/anneliese rothenberger/carlo cossutta/
sherill milnes/tugomir franc/frederick guthrie/siegfried rudolf
frese/mario guggia/ewald aichberger

114/7 september 1971/wiener staatsoper
wagner tannhäuser/conductor berislav klobucar
cd: opera depot OD 10023/premiere 2343

leonie rysanek/gertrude prob-prandl/rita streich/hans beirer/eberhard
waechter/gerd nienstedt/karl terkal/reid bunger/kurt equiluz/frederick
guthrie

115/3 october 1971/guest performance in moscow bolshoi theatre
strauss der rosenkavalier/conductor Josef krips
lp: melodiya C10 28033-28037
cd: voce della luna VL 2001-2003/premiere 1620

leonie rysanek/christa ludwig/hilde de groote/manfred jungwirth/erich kunz/william blankenship/murray dickie/margarita lilowa/emmy loose/ herbert lackner/harald pröglhöf/siegfried rudolf frese/ljubomir pantscheff/karl terkal/laurence dutoit/ewald aichberger

116/20 november 1971/wiener staatsoper
massenet manon/conductor serge baudo
cd: di stefano GDS 21044/myto MCD 91649/opera lovers 197101

Jeannette pilou/giacomo aragall/wladmiro ganzarolli/gianpiero mastromei/ heinz zednik/erland hagegard/hilde de groote/rohangiz yachmi/gertrude jahn/laurence dutoit/alois pernerstorfer/ljubomir pantscheff

117/25 december 1971/wiener staatsoper
verdi la traviata/conductor josef krips
lp: estro armonico EA 003
cd: arkadia CDMP 462/premiere 1188/opera lovers 197101

Ileana cotrubas/nicolai gedda/cornell macneil/emmy loose/edita gruberova/kurt equiluz/ernst gutstein/harald pröglhöf/herbert lackner/mario guggia/ljubomir pantscheff/rudolf resch

118/31 january 1972/wiener staatsoper
cherubini medea/conductor horst stein
cd: melodram CDM 27087/rca-bmg 74321 795952/
opera lovers 197201

leonie rysanek/lucia popp/margarita lilowa/bruno prevedi/nicolai ghiuselev/reid bunger/edita gruberova/laurence dutoit

119/28 may 1972/wiener staatsoper
weber der freischütz/conductor karl böhm
cd: arkadia CDMP 457/foyer 502.059/orfeo C732 072

gundula janowitz/renate holm/james king/eberhard waechter/manfred jungwirth/karl ridderbusch/franz crass/Heinz zednik/gustav elger

120/16 june 1972/wiener staatsoper
verdi don carlo/conductor silvio varviso
cd: house of opera CDBB 630

placido domingo/sena jurinac/christa ludwig/nicolai ghiuselev/piero cappuccilli/otto wiener/herbert lackner/edita gruberova/ewald aichberger/arleen auger/christa reichert

121/27 september 1972/wiener staatsoper
verdi rigoletto/conductor heinz wallberg
cd: premiere 1921

cornell macneil/giacomo aragall/lucia popp/reid bunger/ljubomir pantscheff/milkana nikolova/siegfried rudolf frese/mario guggia/tugomir franc/biserka cvejic/dagmar hermann/laurence dutoit/harald pröglhöf

122/16 october 1972/wiener staatsoper
janacek jenufa/conductor janos kulka/*sung in german*
lp: estro armonico EA 061

sena jurinac/astrid varnay/hilde rössel-majdan/jean cox/william cochran/reid bunger/frederick guthrie/hilde konetzni/hilde de groote/ruthilde boesch/edita gruberova/margarete sjoestedt/milkana nikolova

123/22 december 1972/wiener staatsoper
strauss salome/conductor karl böhm
cd: rca-bmg 74321 694302/74321 694282/opera d'oro 7004

leonie rysanek/grace hofmann/eberhard waechter/hans hopf/waldemar kmentt/rohangiz yachmi/murray dickie/heinz zednik/kurt equiluz/karl terkal/herbert lackner/peter wimberger/siegfried rudolf frese/tugomir franc/frederick guthrie/reid bunger/ewald aichberger

124/4 february 1973/wiener staatsoper
verdi aida/conductor riccardo muti
cd: bella voce BLV 107.209

gwyneth jones/viorica cortez/placido domingo/eugene holmes/bonaldo giaotti/tugomir franc/eduardo alvares/sona ghazarian

125/7 february 1973/wiener staatsoper
verdi rigoletto/conductor georges singer
cd: house of opera HO 901/opera depot OD 10131

kostas paskalis/placido domingo/edda moser/liselotte maikl/reid bunger/ljubomir pantscheff/siegfried rudolf frese/kurt equiluz/tugomir franc/marga schiml/gildis flossmann/anny felbermayer/harald pröglhöf

126/12 february 1973/wiener staatsoper
puccini turandot/conductor berislav klobucar
cd: opera lovers 197301

liane synek/lotte rysanek/james king/kurt equiluz/tugomir franc/hans braun/
robert kerns/heinz zednik/murray dickie/georg ditl

127/6 march 1973/wiener staatsoper
gounod faust/conductor ernst märzendorfer
cd: live rare opera LRO 280/omega opera archive 4416

franco bonisolli/bonaldo giaiotti/Jeannette pilou/kostas paskalis/hans
christian/hilde de groote/hilde rössel-majdan

128/12 september 1973/wiener staatsoper
verdi un ballo in maschera/conductor anton guadagno
cd; lyric distribution 255/omega opera archive OOA 4148

leonie rysanek/biserka cvejic/olivera miljakovic/ludovic spiess/giuseppe
taddei/herbert lackner/frederick guthrie/siegfried rudolf frese/
mario guggia/kurt equiluz

129/7 october 1973/wiener staatsoper
wagner tristan und isolde/conductor carlos kleiber
cd: exclusive EX92 T18-20/as-disc NAS 2511-2513/
phoenix PHE 6601-6603

catarina ligendza/ruza baldani/hans hopf/gustav neidlinger/hans sotin/
hans helm/horst nitsche/anton dermota/georg tichy

130/29 december 1973/wiener staatsoper
puccini la boheme/conductor anton guadagno
cd: opera lovers 197302

ileana cotrubas/lotte rysanek/franco bonisolli/giuseppe taddei/reid bunger/bonaldo giaotti/erich kunz/hans christian/ewald aichberger/ wolfgang ferschl/alexander maly/herbert gnauer

131/3 january 1974/wiener staatsoper
verdi il trovatore/conductor anton guadagno
cd: omega opera archive OOA 4009

lotte rysanek/ruth hesse/pedro lavirgen/giuseppe taddei/bonaldo giaotti/laurence dutoit/siegfried rudolf frese/kurt equiluz/ nikolaus simkowsky

132/21 january 1974/wiener staatsoper
verdi luisa miller/conductor alberto erede
cd: ponto 1009/opera lovers 197401

lilian sukis/christa ludwig/milkana nikolova/franco bonisolli/malcolm smith/bonaldo giaotti/giuseppe taddei/horst nitsche

133/28 january 1974/wiener staatsoper
verdi rigoletto/conductor walter weller
cd: premiere 1017/omega opera archive 3277

bruno pola/jose carreras/reri grist/peter wimberger/ljubomir pantscheff/ liselotte maikl/siegfried rudolf frese/kurt equiluz/Frederick guthrie/unni rugtvegt/anny felbermayer/laurence dutoit/hans braun

134/21 april 1974/wiener staatsoper
mozart don giovanni/conductor leopold hager
cd: premiere 2339/opera depot OD 10122

cesare siepi/gwyneth jones/lotte rysanek/helen donath/luigi alva/karl ridderbusch/enrico fissure/heinz holecek

135/21 june 1974/wiener staatsoper
verdi otello/conductor alberto erede
cd: omega opera archive 5017

james king/teresa zylis-gara/sandor solyom-nagy/rohangiz yachmi/giuseppe zampieri/ewald aichberger/malcolm smith/hans christian/georg tichy

136/29 september 1974/wiener staatsoper
verdi la forza del destino/conductor riccardo muti
cd: myto 043.294/opera lovers 197401/premiere 1036

gilda cruz-romo/joy davidson/franco bonisolli/kostas paskalis/cesare siepi/manfred jungwirth/sesto bruscantini/axelle gall/harald pröglhöf/kurt equiluz/georg tichy

137/2 february 1975/wiener staatsoper
verdi otello/conductor heinz wallberg
cd: house of opera CDBB 738

hans beirer/kostas paskalis/gwyneth jones/margarita lilowa/william blankenship/ewald aichberger/frederick guthrie/siegfried rudolf frese/georg tichy

138/19 september 1975/wiener staatsoper
verdi don carlo/conductor anton guadagno
cd: house of opera OD 10133/premiere 1227

jon vickers/cesare siepi/franco bordoni/gwyneth jones/eva randova/otto wiener/alfred sramek/horst nitsche/olga warla/liselotte maikl/christa reichert

139/21 october 1975/wiener staatsoper
wagner die meistersinger von nürnberg/christoph von dohnanyi
cd: ponto 1006

karl ridderbusch/kurt moll/gundula janowitz/gertrude jahn/james king/ heinz zednik/peter van der bilt/raimund wolansky/karl terkal/hans helm/ horst nitsche/anton wendler/ewald aichberger/harald pröglhöf/alfred sramek/alois pernerstorfer/peter wimberger

140/19 november 1975/wiener staatsoper
verdi il trovatore/conductor ralf weikert
cd: opera lovers 197503

franco bonisolli/gianpiero mastromei/katia ricciarelli/bojka kossewa/franco ventriglia/laurence dutoit/siegfried rudolf frese/nikolaus simkowsky/ horst nitsche

141/4 may 1976/wiener staatsoper
verdi otello/conductor heinz wallberg
cd: house of opera HO 741/opera lovers 197603

franco bonisolli/giuseppe taddei/anna alexieva/czeslawa slania/adolf dallapozza/ewald aichberger/frederick guthrie/siegfried rudolf frese/ christen tichy

142/1 september 1976/wiener staatsoper
verdi don carlo/conductor miguel gomez martinez
cd: opera lovers 197603

giacomo aragall/nicolai ghiaurov/piero cappuccilli/montserrat caballe/
josephine veasey/bengt rundgren/peter wimberger/olga warla/ewald
aichberger/edita gruberova/christa reichert

143/15 october 1976/wiener staatsoper
wagner das rheingold/conductor horst stein
cd: opera depot OD 10185

theo adam/grace hofmann/zoltan kelemen/reid bunger/josef hopferwieser/
peter hofmann/heinz zednik/karl ridderbusch/bengt rundgren/hannelore
bode/margarita lilowa/lotte rysanek/rohangiz yachmi/axelle gall

144/17 october 1976/wiener staatsoper
berlioz les troyens/conductor gerd albrecht
cd: gala GL 100 609

christa ludwig/helga dernesch/guy chauvet/wolfgang schöne/judith
holzmeister/michael weber/olga warla/sona ghazarian/ewald aichberger/
milkana nikolova/alfred sramek/peter wimberger/tugomir franc/horst
laubenthal/margarita lilowa/nicolai ghiuselev/georg tichy/

145/10 november 1976/wiener staatsoper
verdi un ballo in maschera/conductor giuseppe patane
cd: lyric distribution 611

leonie rysanek/fiorenza cossotto/reri grist/giorgio merighi/yuri mazurok/
manfred jungwirth/peter wimberger/georg tichy/dimiter usunow/
ewald aichberger

146/20 november 1976/wiener staatsoper
strauss ariadne auf naxos/conductor karl böhm
cd: private edition vienna

gundula janowitz/agnes baltsa/edita gruberova/james king/erich kunz/
walter berry/peter weber/heinz zednik/georg tichy/alfred sramek/
barry mcdaniel/kurt equiluz/manfred jungwirth/gerhard unger/
hilde de groote/axelle gall/sona ghazarian

147/5 december 1976/wiener staatsoper
wagner tristan und isolde/conductor horst stein
cd: myto MCD 021.257/omega opera archive OOA 3680/
house of opera HO 3755/premiere 2532

birgit nilsson/ruth hesse/jon vickers/hans sotin/hans günter nöcker/
reid bunger/anton dermota/gerhard stolze/harald pröglhöf

148/13 december 1976/wiener staatsoper
puccini tosca/conductor horst stein
cd: premiere 366

montserrat caballe/carlo bergonzi/gianpiero mastromei/reid bunger/
manfred jungwirth/dimiter usunow/herald pröglhöf/helmut
reitschütz/ljubomir pantscheff/margareta hintermeier

149/20 december 1976/wiener staatsoper
puccini tosca/conductor horst stein
cd: house of opera CDBB 445/opera lovers 197605

montserrat caballe/carlo bergonzi/kostas paskalis/reid bunger/manfred
jungwirth/dimiter usunow/harald pröglhöf/helmut reischütz/ljubomir
pantscheff/margareta hintermeier

150/14 march 1977/wiener staatsoper
puccini tosca/conductor alberto erede
cd: myto MCD 014.249/premiere 1940

eva marton/giacomo aragall/kostas paskalis/reid bunger/manfred
jungwirth/dimiter usunow/harald pröglhöf/helmut reischütz/
rudolf kostas/czeslawa slania

151/17 march 1977/wiener staatsoper
bellini norma/conductor riccardo muti
cd: exclusive EX93 T 78-79/live rare opera LRO 248/
serenissima 369 179-180/private edition vienna

montserrat caballe/fiorenza cossotto/carlo cossutta/luigi roni/czeslawa slania/ewald aichberger

152/30 march 1977/televised performance in wiener staatsoper
donizetti don pasquale/conductor hector urbon
dvd: premiere 5048

edita gruberova/luigi alva/hans helm/oskar czerwenka/alois pernserstorfer

153/8 may 1977/wiener staatsoper
verdi il trovatore/conductor herbert von karajan
cd: artists' live recordings FED 002-003/serenissima 360 131-132/
premiere 1241/house of opera CDBB 677/private edition vienna
private edition vienna dated 15 may 1977

leontyne price/christa ludwig/luciano pavarotti/piero cappuccilli/jose van dam/maria venuti/heinz zednik/karl caslavsky/ewald aichberger

154/10 may 1977/wiener staatsoper
mozart le nozze di figaro/conductor herbert von karajan
cd: private edition vienna/orfeo C856 123

jose van dam/tom krause/anna tomowa-sintov/Ileana cotrubas/frederica von stade/jules bastin/heinz zednik/jane berbie/janet perry/kurt equiluz/zoltan kelemen

155/13 may 1977/wiener staatsoper
puccini la boheme/conductor herbert von karajan
cd: private edition vienna/lyric distribution 094

mirella freni/renate holm/jose carreras/rolando panerai/paolo washington/gianni maffeo/claudio giombi/franco calabrese/saverio porzano/nikolaus simkowsky/friedrich strack/willem reyso

156/11 october 1977/wiener staatsoper
strauss elektra/conductor horst stein
cd: opera depot OD 10259

ursula schröder-feinen/christa ludwig/gwyneth jones/theo adam/hans beirer/frederick guthrie/axelle gall/margarethe bence/karl terkal/alois pernerstorfer/szofia peterdy/gertrude jahn/milkana nikolova/lotte rysanek

157/23 and 27 october 1977 (montage)/wiener staarsoper
strauss die frau ohne schatten/conductor karl böhm
lp: historical recording enterprises HRE 322/deutsche grammophon 415 4731
cd: deutsche grammophon 415 4732/445 3252/445 4912

leonie rysanek/birgit nilsson/ruth hesse/james king/walter berry/peter wimberger/lotte rysanek/gertrude jahn/ewald aichberger/hans helm/lorenzo alvary/murray dickie

158/2 december 1977/wiener staatsoper
verdi un ballo in maschera/conductor miguel gomez martinez
cd: myto MCD 033.280/omega opera archive 5592

liliana molnar-talacic/stefania toczyska/sally arneson/nicolai gedda/sherill milnes/peter wimberger/frederick guthrie/peter weber/horst nitsche/franco careccia

159/24 january 1978/televised performance in wiener staatsoper
beethoven fidelio/leonard bernstein
vhs video: great performances (usa) 7
dvd: deutsche grammophpn 073 4159

gundula janowitz/lucia popp/rene kollo/adolf dallapozza/manfred jungwirth/hans sotin/hans helm/karl terkal/alfred sramek

160/10 march 1978/wiener staatsoper
verdi rigoletto/conductor giuseppe patane
cd: opera lovers 197801

matteo manuguerra/alfredo kraus/Ileana cotrubas/milkana nikolova/ peter wimberger/hans christian/rudolf kostas/horst nitsche/tugomir franc/margarita lilowa/anny felbermayer/silvia herman/hans braun

161/23 march 1978/wiener staatsoper
donizetti lucia di lammermoor/conductor giuseppe patane
lp: historical recording enterprises HRE 297
cd: myto MCD 002.217/opera lovers 197801

edita gruberova/czeslawa slania/peter dvorsky/matteo manuguerra/ thomas moser/siegfried vogel/christopher doig

162/1 may 1978/televised performance in wiener staatsoper
verdi il trovatore/conductor herbert von karajan
cd: rca-bmg 74321 619512/74321 619532/premiere 819/
house of opera CDBB 671/opera lovers 197801
dvd: tdk DV-CLOPIT

placido domingo/piero cappuccilli/raina kabaiwanska/fiorenza coddotto/
jose van dam/maria venuti/heinz zednik/karl caslavsky/ewald aichberger

163/6 may 1978/wiener staatsoper
donizetti lucia di lammermoor/conductor giuseppe patane
cd: opera lovers 197802

sona ghazarian/alfredo kraus/rolando panerai/thomas moser/paolo
washington/czeslawa slania/saverio porzani

164/1 september 1978/wiener staatsoper
donizetti lucia di lammermoor/conductot giuseppe patane
cd: premiere 260/encore CD 104/opera lovers 197803

edita gruberova/margarete hintermeier/jose carreras/yuri mazurok/
thomas moser/kurt rydl/christopher doig

165/12 september 1978/wiener staatsoper
strauss der rosenkavalier/conductor reinhard schwarz
cd: opera addiction

gundula janowitz/brigitte fassbaender/lucia popp/manfred jungwirth/hans helm/liselotte maikl/murray dickie/margarita lilowa/peter wimberger/kurt equiluz/ewald aichberger/hans christian/yordi ramiro/elfriede tomek/ karl terkal

166/23 november 1978/wiener staatsoper
rossini il barbiere di siviglia/conductor carlo felice cillario
lp: legendary recordings LR 107
cd: opera lovers 197801

bernd weikl/francisco araiza/agnes baltsa/czeslawa slania/enrico fissore/ tugiomir franc/reid bunger/karl kaslavsky/peter weber

167/9 december 1978/televised performance in wiener staatsoper
bizet carmen/conductor carlos kleiber
cd: golden melodram GM 60003/exclusive EX92 T 11-12/ japan ROP 3/opera d'oro CA 010-011/opera lovers 197801
laserdisc: japan RCS 0696
dvd: tdk CLOPCAR

elena obrazstowa/lsobel buchanan/placido domingo/yuri mazurok/cheryl kanfoush/axelle gall/kurt rydl/hans helm/heinz zednik/paul wolfrum

168/11 february 1979/wiener staatsoper
puccini il trittico/conductor gerd albrecht
cd: orfeo C768 093/opera lovers 197901 (il tabarro only)/
bella voce BLV 107 406 (il tabarro and sour angelica only)

suor angelica: pilar lorengar/kerstin meyer/margarethe bence/axelle gall/
czeslawa slania/olivera miljakovic/maria venuti

il tabarro: renato bruson/marilyn zschau/vladimir atlantov/heinz zednik/
alfred sramek/czeslawa slania/waltraud winsauer/horst nitsche/
michele fiotta

gianni schicchi: walter berry/sona ghazarian/margarita lilowa/yordi ramiro/
heinz zednik/cheryl kanfoush/hans kraemmer/rudolf mazzola/alfred sramek/
marjana lipovsek/erich kunz/paul wolfrum/rudolf kostas/walter fink

169/4 march 1979/wiener staatsoper
puccini la fanciulla del west/conductor giuseppe patane
cd: house of opera CDBB 410

radmila bakocevic/placido domingo/giuseppe taddei/waltraud winsauer/
mario guggia/reid bunger/peter weber/karl terkal/rudolf kostas/horst
nitsche/kurt equiluz/christopher doig/alfred sramek/paul wolfrum/
johann reautschnigg/peter wimberger/jose castro/michele fiotta

170/18 march 1979/wiener staatsoper
wagner parsifal/conductor horst stein
cd: house of opera HO 3607

siegfried jerusalem/leonie rysanek/karl ridderbusch/walter berry/kurt rydl/gertrude jahn/margarete hintermeier/kurt equiluz/chigusa tomita/ thomas moser/rudolf mazzola/patricia wise/hiroko shiraishi/waltraud winsauer/marjorie vance/silvia herman/marjana lipovsek

171/6 may 1979/wiener staatsoper
verdi don carlo/conductor herbert von karajan
cd: premiere 2110/orfeo C816 133

jose carreras/mirella freni/agnes baltsa/ruggiero raimondi/piero cappuccilli/matti salminen/edita gruberova/marjon lambricks/ luigi roni/ewald aichberger

172/9 september 1979/concert performance in wiener staatsoper
mercadante il giuramento/conductor gerd albrecht
lp: historical recording enterprises HRE 319
cd: house of opera CDBB 335/orfeo C680 062

placido domingo/mara zampieri/agnes baltsa/robert kerns/michele fiotta/silvia herman

173/31 december 1979/televised performance in wiener staatsoper
johann strauss die fledermaus/conductor theodor guschlbauer
dvd: arthaus musik 107 153

lucia popp/edita gruberova/brigitte fassbaender/bernd weikl/erich kunz/ josef hopferwieser/walter berry/anton wendler/karin göstling/helmuth lohner/karl caslavsky

174/30 january 1980/wiener staatsoper
verdi la traviata/conductor alberto erede
cd: opera lovers 198002

edda moser/franco bonisolli/eberhard waechter/margarete sjoestedt/cheryl kanfousch/yoshihisa yamaji/Gottfried hornik/peter weber/frederick guthrie/ michele fiotta/franz riedl/rudolf kostas

175/24 february 1980/wiener staatsoper
verdi falstaff/conductor georg solti
cd: legato SRO 587

guillermo sarabia/bernd weikl/yordi ramiro/pilar lorengar/christa ludwig/ sona ghazarian/alexandrina miltschewa/wilfied gahmlich/rudolf mazzola/heinz zednik

176/4 september 1980/wiener staatsoper
verdi la forza del destino/conductor miguel gomez martinez
lp: legendary recordings LR 165

anna tomova-sintow/stefania toczyska/jose carreras/yuri mazurok/peter wimberger/margareta hintermeier/kurt moll/reid bunger/paul wolfrum/ kurt equiluz/neven balamaric

177/23 september 1980/wiener staatsoper
verdi la traviata/conductor gianfranco masini
lp: legendary recordings LR 161

edita gruberova/jose carreras/bernd weikl/gabriele sima/margareta hintermeier/yoshihisa yamaji/reid bunger/neven belamaric/alfred sramek/horst nitsche/elmar breneis/walter fink

178/30 september 1980/televised guest performance in tokyo
mozart le nozze di figaro/conductor karl böhm
cd: eclogue (japan) ECL 1003/discovery RED 129
vhs video: lyric distribution 1097

gundula janowitz/lucia popp/agnes baltsa/bernd weikl/hermann prey/ heinz zednik/kurt rydl/margarita lilowa/maria venuti

179/21 december 1980/wiener staatsoper
verdi attila/conductor giuseppe sinopoli
cd: living stage LS 34720/gala GL 100 592/cin-cin 1012-1013/
orfeo C601 032

nicolai ghiaurov/mara zampieri/piero visconti/piero cappuccilli/
josef hopferwieser/alfred sramek

180/30 april 1981/televised performance in wiener staatsoper
giordano andrea chenier/conductor nello santi
dvd: deutsche grammophon 073 4070

placido domingo/gabriela benackova/piero cappuccilli/rohangiz yachmi/czeslawa slania/fedora barbieri/hans helm/paul wolfrum/reid bunger/alfred sramek/ yoshihisa yamaji/heinz zednik/walter fink/rudolf mazzola

181/22 october 1981/wiener staatsoper
rossini la cenerentola/conductor roberto abbado
cd: premiere

agnes baltsa/francisco araiza/enzo dara/giuseppe taddei/renate holm/gertude jahn/rudolf mazzola

182/25 april 1982/televised performance in wiener staatsoper
smetana the bartered bride/conductor adam fischer/
sung in german
dvd: deutsche grammophon 073 4380

lucia popp/siegfried jerusalem/karl ridderbusch/erich kunz/alfred sramek/ gertrude jahn/walter fink/czeslawa slania/heinz zednik/gabriele sima/ hans christian

183/5 june 1982/wiener staatsoper
verdi otello/conductor james levine
cd: house of opera CDBB 810

placido domingo/mirella freni/cornell macneil/margarita lilowa/thomas moser/horst nitsche/kurt rydl/reid bunger/rudolf kostas

184/29 june 1982/wiener staatsoper
donizetti lucia di lammermoor/conductor hans graf
cd: live rare opera

edita gruberova/franco bonisolli/hans helm/peter wimberger/yoshihisa yamaji/czeslawa slania/gregor caban

185/3 september 1982/wiener staatsoper
verdi la traviata/conductor nello santi
cd: cin-cin 1010-1011

edita gruberova/jose carreras/leo nucci/gabriele sima/margareta hintermeier/
kurt equiluz/georg tichy/noel ramirez/alfred sramek/horst nitsche/elmar
breneis/charles Naylor

186/16 october 1982/wiener staatsoper
wagner tannhäuser/conductor lorin maazel
cd: opera lovers 198201

reiner goldberg/spas wenkoff/anna tomova-sintow/dunja vezjovic/theo adam/
bernd weikl/thomas moser/peter wimberger/kurt equiluz/friedemann hanke/
gabriele sima

187/2 february 1983/wiener staatsoper
verdi falstaff/conductor lorin maazel
cd: opera lovers 198301

walter berry/giorgio zancanaro/francisco araiza/patricia wise/pilar lorengar/
christa ludwig/alexandrina miltschewa/wilfried gahmlich/rudolf mazzola/
heinz zednik

188/16 march 1983/wiener staatsoper
verdi rigoletto/conductor riccardo muti
cd: opera lovers 198301

renato bruson/franco bonisolli/edita gruberova/peter wimberger/hans christian/graciela de gyldenfeldt/charles naylor/helmut wildhaber/john paul bogart/rohangiz yachmi/waltraud winsauer/gabriele sima/ alexander maly

189/14 april 1983/wiener staatsoper
giordano andrea chenier/conductor riccardo chailly
lp: historical recordings enterprises HRE 431

jose carreras/giorgio zancanaro/eva marton/rohangiz yachmi/czeslawa slania/margarita lilowa/gottfried hornik/francisco valls/reid bunger/ alfred sramek/anton wendler/heinz zednik/walter fink/friedemann hanke/rudolf mazzola

190/2 may 1983/wiener staatsoper
strauss capriccio/conductor heinrich hollreiser
cd: opera addiction

gundula janowitz/christa ludwig/peter schreier/hans helm/gottfried hornik/theo adam/waldemar kmentt/ulrike steinsky/helmut wildhaber/rudolf mazzola

191/12 june 1983/televised performance in wiener staatsoper
puccini turandot/conductor lorin maazel
dvd: opera lovers DVDTURA 198301/arthaus 109 094

eva marton/katia ricciarelli/jose carreras/john paul bogart/waldemar
kmentt/kurt rydl/robert kerns/helmut wildhaber/Heinz zednik/
bela perencz

192/1-9 september 1983/montage of three performances
puccini turandot/ conductor lorin maazel
lp: sony M2K 39160
cd: sony SM2K 90444

eva marton/katia ricciarelli/jose carreras/john paul bogart/waldemar
kmentt/kurt rydl/robert kerns/helmut wildhaber/heinz zednik/
bela perencz

193/21 september 1983/wiener staatsoper
verdi il trovatore/conductor charles mackerras
cd: cin-cin 1006-1007

ghena dimitrova/mariana paunova/nicola martinucci/giorgio zancanaro/
john paul bogart/joanna borowska/ewald aichberger/bela perencz/
gerhard panzenbock

194/24 october 1983/wiener staatsoper
berg lulu/conductor lorin maazel
cd: rca-bmg 74321 577342

julia migenes/brigitte fassbaender/margareta hintermeier/hans christian/
heinz zednik/theo adam/richard karczykowski/hans hotter/oskar czerwenka/
kurt rydl/helmut wildhaber/franz kasemann/wolfgang müller-lorenz/alfred
sramek/reid bunger/anton wendler/ulrike steinsky/margarethe bence/
axelle gall/georg tichy/charles naylor

195/8 december 1983/televised performance in wiener staatsoper
massenet manon/conductor adam fischer
dvd: deutsche grammophon 073 4207

edita gruberova/francisco araiza/pierre thau/hans helm/wilfried gahmlich/
georg tichy/donna robin/margareta hintermeier/axelle gall/margarethe
bence/alfred sramek/helge brunner

196/18 january 1984/televised performance in wiener staatsoper
bizet carmen/conductor lorin maazel
cd: house of opera CDBB 134
video recording remains unpublished

agnes baltsa/faith esham/placido domingo/ruggero raimondi/graciela de gyldenfeldt/margarete hintermeier/kurt rydl/hans helm/helmut wildhaber/heinz holecek

197/22 march 1984/wiener staatsoper
verdi simon boccanegra/conductor claudio abbado
cd: rca-bmg 74321 577332

renato bruson/ruggero raimondi/katia ricciarelli/veriano luchetti/felice schiavi/konstantin sfiris/ewald aichberger/anna gonad

198/6 november 1984/wiener staatsoper
strauss die frau ohne schatten/conductor christoph von dohnanyi
cd: premiere 2369

leonie rysanek/gwyneth jones/ruth hesse/james king/walter berry/robert kerns/lotte rysanek/john dickie/marjorie vance/gertrude jahn/georg tichy/rudolf mazzola/helmut wildhaber

199/4 january 1985/wiener staatsoper
wagner lohengrin/conductor peter schneider
cd: premiere 2208/house of opera CDBB 945

placido domingo/catarina ligendza/leonie rysanek/hermann becht/peter wimberger/georg tichy/franz kasemann/anton wendler/Alexander maly/jaroslav stajnc

200/16 march 1985/televised performance in wiener staatsoper
gounod faust/conductor erich binder
dvd: deutsche grammophon 073 4108

francisco araiza/ruggero raimondi/gabriele benackova/gabriele sima/gertrude jahn/walton grönroos/alfred sramek

201/6 june 1985/wiener staatsoper
leoncavallo pagliacci/conductor adam fischer
cd: premiere 1179/orfeo C756 081

placido domingo/ileana cotrubas/matteo maneguerra/heinz zednik/wolfgang schöne/Josef pogatschnig/wolfgang witte

202/24 may 1986/televised performance in wiener staatsoper
ponchielli la gioconda/conductor adam fischer
cd: house of opera CDBB 370
laserdisc: pioneer PLMCC 00611
dvd: arthaus 100 232

eva marton/ludmilla semtschuk/placido domingo/matteo manuguerra/
kurt rydl/margarita lilowa/alfred sramek/alfred burgstaller/Jorge pita/
goran simic/benedikt kobel/peter koves/francisco valls

203/22 october 1986/televised performance in wiener staatsoper
verdi un ballo in maschera/conductor claudio abbado
cd: house of opera CDWW 985/legato LCD 236/
serenissima 360 118-119
video recording remains unpublished

gabriele lechner/ludmilla semtschuk/luciano pavarotti/piero cappuccilli/
magda nador/franco de grandis/goran simic/georg tichy/alexander
maly/franz kasemann

204/10 april 1987/wiener staatsoper
dvorak rusalka/conductor vaclav neumann
cd: orfeo C638 042

gabriela benackova/eva randova/peter dvorsky/evgeny nesterenko/alexander maly/margarete hintermeier/noriko sasaki/gabriele sima

205/10 may 1987/wiener staatsoper
verdi otello/conductor zubin mehta
cd: house of opera CDBB 786/orfeo C098 072

placido domingo/renato bruson/anna tomowa-sinov/margarita lilowa/kaludi kaludow/wilfried gahmlich/kurt rydl/goran simic/peter koves

206/17 may 1987/wiener staatsoper
verdi otello/conductor zubin mehta
cd: house of opera CDBB 787

placido domingo/renato bruson/anna tomowa=sintov/margarita lilowa/kaludi kaludow/wilfried gahmlich/kurt rydl/goran simic/peter koves

207/28 may 1987/wiener staatsoper
verdi un ballo in maschera/conductor claudio abbado
cd: house of opera CDBB 927

maria chiara/ludmilla semtschuk/placido domingo/piero cappuccilli/patricia pace/alfred sramek/goran simic/claudio otelli/alexander maly/
franz kasemann

208/11 june 1987/wiener staatsoper
verdi otello/conductor adam fischer
cd: house of opera CDBB 733

vladimir atlantov/gabriela benackova/sherill milnes/margareta hintermeier/
kaludi kaludow/kurt rydl/goran simic/peter koves

209/28 september 1987/wiener staatsoper
rossini l'italiana in algeri/conductor claudio abbado
cd: opera lovers 198701

agnes baltsa/frank lopardo/alessandro corbelli/ruggiero raimondi/patrizia pace/anna gonad/enzo dara

210/11 january 1988/wiener staatsoper
puccini tosca/conductor garcia navarro
cd: opera lovers 198801

ghena dimitrova/peter dvorsky/giuseppe taddei/gottfried hornik/rudolf mazzola/helmut wildhaber/hans christian/goran simic

211/11 may 1988/wiener staatsoper
verdi otello/conductor adam fischer
cd: premiere 175/house of opera CDBB 730

vladimir atlantov/renato bruson/aprile millo/margarita lilowa/kaludi kaludow/ helmut wildhaber/kurt rydl/goran simic/peter koves

212/16 may 1988/wiener staatsoper
tchaikovsky evgeny onegin/conductor seiji ozawa
cd: orfeo C637 042

wolfgang brendel/mirella freni/peter dvorsky/gertrude jahn/rohangiz yachmi/ margarita lilowa/nicolai ghiaurov/peter koves/robert kerns/heinz zednik/peter jelosits

213/20 november 1988/wiener staatsoper
wagner tannhäuser/conductor giuseppe sinopoli
cd: opera addiction OA 2450

richard versalle/sharon sweet/waltraud meier/andreas schmidt/kurt rydl/
richard burke/john antoniou/peter jelosits/goran simic/noriko sasaki

214/21 january 1989/televised performance in wiener staatsoper
mussorgsky khovantschina/conductor claudio abbado
dvd: arthaus 100 310/pioneer PLMCC 00631/
opera lovers DVDKHO 198901

nicolai ghiaurov/vladimir atlantov/ludmilla semtschuk/yuri masurin/anatoly kotscherga/paata burchuladze/brigitte poschner-klebel/Joanna borowska/ peter koves/wilfried gahmlich/timothy breese/goran simic/bojidar nikolov/heinz zednik

215/8 february 1989/wiener staatsoper
verdi otello/conductor adam fischer
cd: house of opera CDBB 822

placido domingo/franz grundheber/linda plech/margarita lilowa/richard burke/kurt rydl/wilfried gahmlich/goran simic

216/12-14 february 1989/wiener staatsoper
verdi otello/conductor adam fischer
cd: house of opera CDBB 826
it is not clear whether this is two separate performances or a montage from the two dates

placido domingo/franz grundheber/katia ricciarelli/margareta hintermeier/richard burke/kurt rydl/wilfried gahmlich/goran simic

217/19 june 1989/televised performance in wiener staatsoper
strauss elektra/conductor claudio abbado
laserdisc: pioneer PLMCC 800221
dvd: arthaus 100 048

eva marton/brigitte fassbaender/cheryl studer/james king/franz grundheber/goran simic/waltraud winsauer/noriko sasaki/wilfried gahmlich/claudio otelli/gabriele lechner/margarita lilowa/gabriele sima/margareta hintermeier/brigitte poschner-klebel/joanna borowska

218/17-30 september 1989/montage of performances in wiener staatsoper
mussorgsky khovantschina/conductor claudio abbado
cd: deutsche grammophon 429 7582

nicolai ghiaurov/vladimir atlantov/marjana lipovsek/yuri masurin/anatoly kotscherga/paata burchuladze/brigitte poschner-klebel/Joanna borowska/ peter koves/wilfried gahmlich/timothy breese/goran simic/bojidar nikolov/heinz zednik

219/7 october 1989/wiener staatsoper
verdi don carlo/conductor claudio abbado
cd: opera lovers 198901/house of opera CDWW 1025

luis lima/renato bruson/ruggero raimondi/mirella freni/agnes baltsa/ anatolij kotscherga/goran simic/gabriela sima/brigitte poschner-klebel/ bojidar nikolov

220/28 january 1990/televised performance in wiener staatsoper
wagner lohengrin/conductor claudio abbado
laserdisc: pioneer PLMCC 26735
dvd: arthaus 100 956

placido domingo/cheryl studer/dunja vejzovic/hartmut welker/robert lloyd/
eike wilm schulte/bojidar nikolov/franz kasemann/claudio otelli/peter koves

221/22 november 1990/wiener staatsoper
wagner die meistersinger von nürnberg/conductor colin davis
cd: premiere 2511/opera addiction OA 3059

jose van dam/kurt rydl/matti salminen/rudolf hartmann/rene kollo/wilfried
gahmlich/lucia popp/rohangiz yachmi/richard decker/john antoniou/walter
berry/franz kasemann/anton wendler/peter jelosits/hans christian/
alexander trauner/jaroslav stajnc/manfred hemm

222/12 may 1991/televised performance by staatsoper im theater
an der wien
mozart le nozze di figaro/conductor claudio abbado
laserdisc: sony S2LV 46406
vhs video: sony SHV 46406

cheryl studer/marie mclaughlin/gabriele sima/lucio gallo/ruggero raimondi/
margarita lilowa/heinz zednik/franz kasemann/rudolf mazzola/istvan
gati/valentina valente

223/30 june 1991/wiener staatsoper
verdi otello/conductor michael schonwandt
cd: house of opera CDBB 828

placido domingo/sherill milnes/katia ricciarelli/margarita lilowa/bernard lombardo/helmut wildhaber/peter koves/goran simic/john antoniou

224/14 september 1991/wiener staatsoper
verdi otello/conductor berislav klobucar
cd: house of opera CDBB 846

giuseppe giacomini/renato bruson/rosalind plowright/margarita lilowa/richard brunner/wilfried gahmlich/poran simic/claudio otelli/nikolaus simkowsky

225/16 september 1991/wiener staatsoper
strauss salome/conductor peter schneider
cd: premiere 1401/opera lovers 199101

mara zampieri/leonie rysanek/monte pederson/horst hiestermann/richard brunner/margarete hintermeier/ernst-dieter suttheimer/peter jelosits/anton wendler/helmut wildhaber/rudolf mazzola/peter wimbeger/claudio otelli/alfred sramek/roland schubert/peter koves/adolf tomaschek/wolfgang pöltner

226/4 january 1992/wiener staatsoper
verdi la traviata/conductor jan latham-koenig
cd: omega opera archive 4918

cheryl studer/alfredo kraus/juan pons/jutta geister/Hedwig witte/bojidar nikolov/istvan gati/jaroslav stajnc/Alfred sramek

227/9-18 february 1992/two performances in wiener staatsoper
verdi otello/conductor jan latham-könig
cd: house of opera CDBB 798 (9 february)/CDBB 797 (18 february)

placido domingo/piero cappuccilli/kallen esperian/margarita lilowa/bojidar nikolov/wilfried gahmlich/rudolf mazzola/istvan gati/nikolaus simkowsky

228/17 september 1992/wiener staatsoper
giordano andrea chenier/conductor marcello viotti
lp: legato LCD 557
cd: premiere 2180/house of opera CDBB 255

giuseppe giacomini/renato bruson/katia ricciarelli/vesselina kasarova/anna gonda/margarita lilowa/hans helm/claudio otelli/goran simic/renato girolami/anton wendler/wilfried gahmlich/dariusz niemirowicz/hans christian/Rudolf mazzola

229/19 december 1992/wiener staatsoper
wagner die walküre/conductor christoph von dohnanyi
cd: house of opera CDBB 957/opera addiction OA 3060

hildegard behrens/waltraud meier/uta priew/placido domingo/robert hale/
kurt rydl/maria russo/Joanna borowska/Julia faulkner/nelly boschkowa/
margarete hintermeier/lioba braun/jutta geister/anna gonda

230/27 march 1993/wiener staatsoper
verdi falstaff/conductor seiji ozawa
cd: opera addiction OA 4686

benjamin luxon/vladimir chernov/ramon vargas/nancy gustafson/angela
gheorghiu/nelly boschkowa/vesslina kasarowa/helmut wildhaber/
wilfried gahmlich/anatolij kotscherga

231/18-21 june 1993/two performances in wiener staatsoper
leoncavallo pagliacci/conductor michael halasz
cd: house of opera CDBB 285 (18 june)/CDBB 286 (21 june)

placido domingo/Joanna borowska/bruno pola/herwig pecoraro/
bo skovhus/adolf tomaschek/gerhard panzenböck

232/21 june 1993/wiener staatsoper
mascagni cavalleria rusticana/conductor michael halasz
cd: premiere 2363

gwyneth jones/bruno sebastian/nelly boschkowa/mark rucker/axelle gall

233/20 december 1993/wiener staatsoper
offenbach les contes d'hoffmann/conductor christian badea
cd: premiere 1181

placido domingo/natalie dessay/barbara frittoli/eliane coelho/bryn terfel/
margarita lilowa/gottfried hornik/herwig pecoraro/roland schubert/peter
koves/heinz zednik/wolfgang bankl/istvan gati

234/9 march 1994/wiener staatsoper
puccini manon lescaut/conductor antonio pappano
cd: opera addiction OA 4077

tiziana fabbricini/kristjan johannsson/jean-luc chaignaud/rudolf mazzola/
ruben broitman/peter koves/graciela araya/helmut wildhaber/benedikt
kobel/dariusz niemirowicz/alfred sramek

235/23 march 1994/televised performance in wiener staatsoper
strauss der rosenkavalier/conductor carlos kleiber
cd: link 601
laserdisc: deutsche grammophon 072 4431
dvd: deutsche grammophon 073 0089

felicity lott/anne sofie von otter/barbara bonney/kurt moll/gottfried hornik/ olivera miljakovic/heinz zednik/anna gonda/keith ikaia-purdy/peter wimberger/ waldemar kmentt/franz kasemann/wolfgang bankl/ingeborg piffl/lotte leitner/ulrich grossrubatscher/peter jelosits

236/2 may 1994/wiener staasoper
bellini i puritani/conductor placido domingo
cd: premiere 1197

edita gruberova/marcello giordani/dimitri hvorostovsky/roberto scandiuzzi/ goran simic/ruben broitman/graciela araya

237/23 may 1994/wiener staatsoper
giordano andrea chenier/conductor marcello viotti
cd: lyric distribution 1011/omega opera archive 4052

giuseppe giacomini/renato bruson/eva marton/graciela araya/anna gonda/ margarita lilowa/yu chen/sebastian holecek/goran simic/alfred sramek/ franz kasemann/wilfried gahmlich/dariusz niemirowiecz/walter zeh/ rudolf mazzola

238/15 december 1994/wiener staatsoper
giordano fedora/conductor fabio luisi
cd: premiere 1178

agnes baltsa/jose carreras/jean-luc chaignaud/ildiko raimondi/svetlana serdar/wilfried gahmlich/ruben broitman/roland schubert/yu chen/ rudolf mazzola/wolfgang bankl

239/2 january 1995/wiener staatsoper
rossini l'italiana in algeri/conductor marcello viotti
cd: house of opera HO 655

viktoria loukianetz/vesselina kasarova/maurizio picconi/raul gimenez/ waltraud winsauer/georg tichy/renato girolami

240/5 january 1995/wiener staatsoper
bizet carmen/conductor donald runnicles
cd: house of opera CDBB 135

agnes baltsa/nancy gustafson/neil schicoff/jean-luc chaignaud/simian ivan/svetlana serdar/goran simic/yu chen/herwig pecoraro/hans peter kammerer/nikolaus simkowsky

241/12 february 1995/wiener staatsoper
massenet herodiade/conductor marcello viotti
cd: rca-bmg 74321 795972/opera lovers 199501

agnes baltsa/placido domingo/juan pons/nancy gustafson/ferruccio furlanetto/
hans helm/david cale johnson/ruben broitman

242/16 february 1995/wiener staatsoper
verdi aida/conductor placido domingo
cd: house of opera CDBB 612

alessandra marc/luciana d'intino/giuseppe giacomini/walter fink/francesco
ellero d'artegna/juan pons/richard brunner/marjorie vance

243/30 march 1995/wiener staatsoper
verdi otello/conductor christian badea
cd: house of opera HO 849

giuseppe giacomini/Julia varady/segei leiferkus/benedikt kobel/margarita
lilowa/peter jelosits/rudolf mazzola/istvan gati/nikolaus simkowsky

244/9 may 1996/wiener staatsoper
verdi otello/conductor donald runnicles
cd: house of opera CDBB 848

giuseppe giacomini/julia varady/renato bruson/benedikt kobel/peter jelosits/
rudolf mazzola/istvan gati/nikolaus simkowsky/margareta hintermeier

245/21-24 february 1997/two performances in wiener staatsoper
verdi otello/conductor michael halasz (21 february)/
daniel oren (24 february)
cd: house of opera CDBB 815 (21 february)/CDBB 721 (24 february)

placido domingo/barbara frittoli/bernd weikl/miro dvorsky/goran simic/wilfried
gahmlich/evgeny dimitriev/nikolaus simkowsky/malgorzata walewska

246/28 may 1997/wiener staatsoper
verdi otello/conductor marcello viotti
cd: house of opera CDBB 840

vladimir galuzin/eliane coelho/renato bruson/benedikt kobel/peter jelosits/
rudolf mazzola/evgeny dimitriev/nikolaus simkowsky/malgorzata walewska

247/29 may 1997/wiener staatsoper
enescu oedipe/conductor michael gielen
cd: naxos 8.660 163-164

monte pederson/egils silins/marjana lipovesek/davide damiani/michael roider/goran simic/peter koves/walter fink/yu chen/Josef hopferwieser/ ruxandra donose/mihaela ungureanu

248/22 june 1997/wiener staatsoper
verdi aida/conductor marcello viotti
cd: house of opera HO 606

deborah voigt/waltraud meier/kristjan johannsson/kurt rydl/simon estes/ david cale johnson/franz kasemann/marjorie vance

249/31 october 1997/wiener staatsoper
verdi otello/conductor adam fischer
cd: house of opera CDBB 839

vladimir galuzine/renato bruson/adrianne pieczonka/torsten kerl/malgorzata walewska/wilfried gahmlich/goran simic/istvan gati/friedrich springer

250/13 december 1997/televised performance in wiener staatsoper
wagner rienzi/conductor zubin mehta
cd: opera addiction OA 4695
dvd: house of opera DVDBB 2964

siegfried Jerusalem/nancy gustafson/violeta urmana/walter fink/peter weber/ roland schubert/torsten kerl/wolfgang bankl/anat efraty

251/5 april 1998/wiener staatsoper
mozart le nozze di figaro/conductor jun märkl
cd: house of opera HO 643

soile isokoski/isabel rey/angelika kirchschlager/bryn terfel/davide damiani/ wilfried gahmlich/gertrude jahn/franz kasemann/franz hawlata/istvan gati/uta schwabe

252/21 may 1998/wiener staatsoper
meyerbeer le prophete/conductor marcello viotti
cd: opera lovers 199801

placido domingo/agnes baltsa/viktotia loukianetz/davide damiani/franz hawlata/david cale johnson/torsten kerl/alexander pinderak/Johannes gisser/albert pesendorfer

253/11 september 1998/wiener staatsoper
strauss ariadne auf naxos/conductor peter schneider
cd: premiere 455

deborah voigt/susan graham/edita gruberova/janez lotric/waldemar kmentt/peter weber/michael kurz/helmut wildhaber/ulrich grossrubatscher/alfred sramek/geert smits/peter jelosits/rudolf mazzola/herwig pecoraro/regina mauel/uta schwabe

254/5 october 1998/wiener staatsoper
verdi rigoletto/conductor michael halasz
cd: house of opera HO 894

georg tichy/aquiles machado/stefania bonfadelli/peter wimberger/aik martirosyan/annely peebo/marian pop/peter jelosits/wojtek smilek/ svetlana serdar/waltraud winsauer

255/24 october 1998/wiener staatsoper
rossini guillaume tell/conductor fabio luisi
cd: orfeo C640 053

thomas hampson/giuseppe sabbatini/nancy gustafson/wojtek smilek/walter fink/dawn kotoski/egils silins/john dickie/mathias zachariassen/yu chen/ mihaela ungureanu/Johannes gasser

256/14 december 1998/wiener staatsoper
verdi ernani/conductor seiji ozawa
cd: house of opera HO 715/premiere 1220

neil shicoff/michele crider/carlos alvarez/roberto scandiuzzi/liliana ciuca/ benedikt kobel/aik martirosyan

257/1 april 1999/wiener staatsoper
wagner parsifal/conductor jun märkl
cd: house of opera HO 559

siegfried Jerusalem/matthias hölle/gabriele schnaut/gottfried hornik/ walter fink/Ingrid kaiserfeld/olga schalaewa/simian ivan/stella grigorian/ uta schwabe/mihaela ungureanu/andrea bönig/linda pavelka/franz kasemann/peter jelosits/benedikt kobel/peter koves

258/29 may 1999/wiener staatsoper
tchaikovsky pique dame/conductor seiji ozawa
cd: house of opera CDBB 585

placido domingo/galina gorchokova/Svetlana serdar/rita gorr/sergei leiferkus/ dmitri hvorostovsky/herwig pecoraro/rudolf mazzola/franz kasemann/marcus pelz/peter jelosits/waltraud winsauer/racel harnisch

259/5 june 1999/wiener staatsoper
verdi ernani/conductor seiji ozawa
cd: house of opera HO 984

neil shicoff/renato bruson/maria guleghina/roberto scandiuzzi/stella grigorian/ benedikt kobel/Marcus pelz

260/27 june 1999/televised staarsoper performance in theater an der wien
mozart don giovanni/conductor riccardo muti
cd: house of opera CDBB 348
dvd: tdk DVWOP DG

carlos alvarez/ildebrando d'arcangelo/adrianne pieczonka/anna caterina antonacci/angelika kirchschlager/michael schade/franz-josef selig/lorenzo regazzo

261/15 october 1999/wiener staatsoper
giordano fedora/conductor anton guadagno
cd: house of opera HO 2426/premiere 736

mara zampieri/franco bonisolli/georg tichy/anat efraty/mihaela ungureanu/john dickie/peter jelosits/alexandru moisuc/yu chen/rudolf mazzola/david cale Johnson/Mario steller/hakki ozpinar/martin thyringer/paul harris/nickolaas van huyssteen

262/23 october 1999/wiener staatsoper
halevy la juive/conductor simone young
cd: rca-bmg 74321 179596/opera lovers 199901

neil shicoff/soile isokoski/regina schörg/alastair miles/zoran todorovich/boaz daniel/janusz monarcha/marcus pelz

263/25 november 1999/wiener staatsoper
puccini la boheme/conductor jun märkl
cd: house of opera CDBB 401

ana maria martinez/maria costanza nocentini/ramon vargas/boaz daniel/
manuel lanza/janusz monarcha/wolfgang bankl/johann reinprecht/
gerhard panzenböck/wolfgang equiluz/peter fraiss

264/11 december 1999/wiener staatsoper
strauss die frau ohne schatten/conductor giuseppe sinopoli
cd: premiere 031363/private edition vienna

deborah voigt/gabriele schnaut/marjana lipovsek/johan botha/falk
struckmann/wolfgang bankl/rachel harnisch/regina mauel/geert
smits/peter koves/herwig pecoraro

265/14 january 2000/wiener staatsoper
puccini tosca/conductor vjekoslav sutej
cd: premiere

eliane coelho/johan botha/falk struckmann/gottfried hornik/alfred
sramek/helmut wildhaber/marcus pelz/stella grigorian

266/6 may 2000/wiener staatsoper
strauss die frau ohne schatten/conductor giuseppe sinopoli
cd: handelman 09253

deborah voigt/gabriele schnaut/jane henschel/ben Heppner/falk struckmann/wolfgang bankl/Rachel harnisch/regina mauel/geert smits/peter koves/herwig pecoraro

267/8-12 october 2000/two performances in wiener staatsoper
wagner tristan und isolde/conductor semyon bychkov
cd: house of opera HO 3734 (8 october)/private edition vienna (8 october)/premiere 2500 (12 october)

gösta winbergh/waltraud meier/mihoko fujimura/peter weber/matti salminen/geert smits/herwig pecoraro/marcus pelz/michael roder

268/25 november 2000/wiener staatsoper
verdi il trovatore/conductor arthur fagen
cd: house of opera HO 717

Janez lotric/georg tichy/ines salazar/elena batoukova/goran simic/stella grigorian/john nuzzo/josef stangl/cosmin ifrim

269/27 january 2001/wiener staatsoper
verdi otello/conductor marcello viotti
cd: house of opera CDBB 759

Jose cura/solie isokoski/renato bruson/john dickie/walter paurisch/rudolf mazzola/istvan gati/hacik bayvertian/margareta hintermeier

270/28 january 2001/wiener staatsoper
verdi aida/conductor fabio luisi
cd: premiere 1189

maria guleghina/waltraud meier/sergei larin/franz grundheber/janusz monarcha/dan paul dimitrescu/michael roider/ricarda merbeth

271/12 february 2001/wiener staatsoper
britten billy budd/conductor donald runnicles
cd: orfeo C602 033

bo skovhus/neil shicoff/eric halfvarson/robert bork/wolfgang bankl/ david cale johnson/john dickie/geert smits/Alfred sramek/john nuzzo/ cosmin ifrim/janusz monarcha/boaz daniel/marcus pelz/peter jelosits/ yu chen/mario steller/valentine heidrich

272/31 may 2001/televised performance in wiener staatsoper
verdi nabucco/conductor fabio luisi
cd: house of opera HO 726
dvd: tdk DVDDVWW-OPNAB

leo nucci/maria guleghina/miro dvorskay/giacomo prestia/marina domashenko/
goran simic/walter pauritsch/renate pitscheider

273/18 june 2001/televised performance in wiener staatsoper
mozart le nozze di figaro/conductor riccardo muti
dvd premiere 6235

melanie diener/tatiana lisnic/angelika kirchschlager/simon keenlyside/carlos
alvarez/francesca pedaci/michael roider/peter jelosits/maurizio muraro/
boaz daniel/Ileana tonca

274/21 september 2001/wiener staatsoper
verdi i vespri siciliani/conductor anton guadagno
cd: house of opera CDBB 660

anthony michaels-moore/nelly miricioiu/janez lotric/ferruccio furlanetto/
wolfgang bankl/liviu burz/stella grigorian/john dickie/john nuzzo/
boaz daniel

275/30 september 2001/wiener staatsoper
bizet carmen/conductor vjekoslav sutej
cd: house of opera HO 152

nadja michael/krassimira stoyanova/stephen o'mara/albert dohmen/
ileana tonca/cornelia salje/peter jelosits/walter pauritsch

276/19 october 2001/wiener staatsoper
bellini la sonnambula/conductor stefano ranzani
cd: live rare opera LRO 241/premiere 1080

stefania bonfadelli/juan diego florez/egils silins/nelly boschkowa/simian ivan/boaz daniel/johann reinprecht

277/3 november 2001/wiener staatsoper
wagner die walküre/conductor peter schneider
cd: house of opera CDBB 959

hildegard behrens/waltraud meier/marjana lipovsek/placido domingo/
jan hendrik rootering/walter fink/karin mann/ricarda merbeth/ingrid kaiserfeld/michelle breedt/stella grigorian/mihaela ungureanu/
svetlana serdar/helene renada

278/11 december 2001/wiener staatsoper
verdi otello/conductor marcello viotti
cd: house of opera CDBB 890

Jon frederic west/jean-philippe lafort/marina mescheriakova/michelle breedt/torsten kerl/walter pauritsch/dan paul dimitrescu/markus nieminen/hacik bayvertian

279/23 january 2002/wiener staatsoper
leoncavallo i pagliacci/conductor adam fischer
cd: live rare opera LRO 439

jose cura/krassimira stoyanova/leo nucci/benedikt kobel/yu chen/gerhard panzenböck/ulrich grossrubatscher

280/24 february 2002/wiener staatsoper
janacek jenufa/conductor seiji ozawa/*sung in german*
cd: private edition vienna

angela denoke/agnes baltsa/jorma silvasti/totsten kerl/anny schlemm/wolfgang bankl/walter fink/helene ranada/renate pitscheider/stella grigorian/cornelia salje/lleana tonca/waltraud winsauer

281/8 april 2002/wiener staatsoper
verdi don carlo/conductor leopold hager
cd: house of opera CDBB 640

keith ikaia-purdy/carlos alvarez/ferruccio furlanetto/carol vanes/larissa diadkova/eric halfvarson/dan paul dimitrescu/florina carmen hinsu/ markus nieminen/Ingrid kaiserfeld

282/7 may 2002/wiener staatsoper
gounod romeo et juliette/conductor marcello viotti
cd: premiere 978

neil shicoff/stefania bonfadelli/michelle breedt/mihaela ungureanu/john dickie/michael knapp/yu chen/markus nieminen/in-sung sim/alfred sramek/walter fink/dan paul dimitrescu

283/9 june 2002/staatsoper im theater an der wien
mozart cosi fan tutte/conductor riccardo muti
cd: private edition vienna

barbara frittoli/angelika kirchschlager/stefania bonfadelli/michael schade/
bo skovhus/alessandro corbelli

284/10 june 2002/wiener staatsoper
donizetti lucia di lammermoor/conductor frederic chaslin
cd: premiere 1203

stefania bonfadelli/tito beltram/manuel lanza/dan paul dimitrescu/john
nuzzio/florina carmen hinsu/cosmin ifrim

285/13-15 june 2002/montage of dress rehearsal and performance
in wiener staatsoper
cerha der riese vom steinfeld/conductor michael boder
cd: austrian radio ORF 662

thomas hampson/diana damrau/michelle breedt/herwig pecoraro/wolfgang
bankl/branko samarowski/alfred sramek/heinz zednik/margareta
hintermeier/benedikt kobel/janusz monarcha

286/18 september 2002/televised performance in wiener staatsoper
donizetti roberto devereux/conductor frederic chaslin
dvd: premiere 5670

edita gruberova/renato bruson/jose bros/enkelejda shkosa/coamin ifrim/
in-sung kim/hiro ijichi

287/14 october 2002/televised performance in wiener staatsoper
verdi simon boccanegra/conductor daniele gatti
cd: premiere 974/house of opera CDBB 917
dvd: tdk DVWW-OPSIBOW

thomas hampson/ferruccio furlanetto/miro dvorsky/boaz daniel/dan paul dimitrescu/cristina gallardo-domas/john nuzzio/songmi yang

288/16 january 2003/wiener staatsoper
gounod romeo et juliette/conductor marcello viotti
cd: premiere 977

marcello giordani/norah amsellem/cornelia salje/mihaela ungureanu/john dickie/christoph levente hara/adrian eröd/markus nieminen/marcus pelz/ alfred sramek/walter fink/janusz monarcha

289/17 february 2003/wiener staatsoper
donizetti la favorita/conductor fabio luisi
cd: premiere 982/opera lovers 200301

violeta urmana/giuseppe sabbatini/carlos alvarez/giacomo prestia/john dickie/genia kühmeier

290/7 may 2003/televised performance in wiener staatsoper
halevy la juive/conductor vjekoslav sutej
dvd: deutsche grammophon 073 4001

neil shicoff/krassimira stoyanova/simian ivan/walter fink/jianvi zhang/ boaz daniel/janusz monarcha/hacik bayvertian/hizo ijichi/martin müller

291/25 may 2003/wiener staatsoper
wagner tristan und isolde/conductor christian thielemann
cd: premiere 1046/private edition vienna

thomas moser/deborah voigt/petra lang/peter weber/robert holl/markus nieminen/michael roider/john dickie/in-sung sim

292/25-29 may 2003/montage of two performances in wiener staatsoper
wagner tristan und isolde/conductor christian thielemann
cd: deutsche grammophon 474 9742

thomas moser/deborah voigt/petra lang/peter weber/robert holl/markus nieminen/michael roider/john dickie/in-sung sim

293/1 june 2003/wiener staatsoper
giordano andrea chenier/conductor adam fischer
cd: premiere 1011

Johan botha/lado ataneli/violeta urmana/elina garanca/margareta hintermeier/mihaela ungureanu/boaz daniel/hans peter kammerer/goran simic/alfred sramek/peter jelosits/herwig pecoraro/peter koves/janusz monarcha

294/2 october 2003/wiener staatsoper
giordano fedora/conductor stefano ranzani
cd: premiere 1294

paoletta marrocu/placiod domingo/georg tichy/bori keszei/antigone papoulkas/cosmin ifrim/peter jelosits/dan paul dimitrescu/adrian eröd/ goran simic/Johannes wiedecke/friedrich springer/ulrich grossrubatscher/ hermann thyringer/jendrik springer/peter leutgöb

295/5 december 2003/wiener staatsoper
wagner der fliegende holländer/conductor seiji ozawa
cd: opera lovers 200301/private edition vienna

falk struckmann/nina stemme/franz hawlata/mihaela ungureanu/ torsten kerl/john dickie

296/14 december 2003/televised performance in wiener staatsoper
wagner der fliegende holländer/conductor seiji ozawa
dvd: premiere 5796/house of opera DVDCC 566/encore 2573

franz grundheber/nina stemme/walter fink/margareta hintermeier/ torsten kerl/john dickie

297/5 february 2004/wiener staatsoper
donizetti la favorite/conductor vjekoslav sutej
cd: premiere 1478

luciana d'intino/ramon vargas/manuel lanza/dan paul dimitrescu/
cosmin ifrim/genia kühmeier

298/2 march 2004/wiener staatsoper
bellini i puritani/conductor stefan soltesz
cd: premiere

stefania bonfadelli/joseph calleja/goran simic/alastair miles/manuel
lanza/benedikt kobel/caitlin hulcup

299/11 april 2004/wiener staatsoper
wagner parsifal/conductor donald runnicles
cd: premiere 1376

johan botha/angela denoke/robert holl/thomas quasthoff/wolfgang
bankl/walter fink/cornelia salje/daniela denschlag/genia kühmeier/
bori keszei/antigone palpoukas/ildiko raimondi/renate pitscheider/
nadia krasteva/arnold bezuyen/peter jelosits/cosmin ifrim/
johannes wiedecke

300/13 june 2004/televised performance in wiener staatsoper
strauss daphne/conductor semyon bychkov
cd: private edition vienna
dvd: encore 2288

ricarda merbeth/marjana lipovsek/michael schade/johan botha/walter fink/markus nieminen/benedikt kobel/jens musger/Johannes wiedecke/genia kühmeier/aarona bogdan

301/27 june 2004/wiener staatsoper
gounod romeo et juliette/conductor marcello viotti
cd: premiere 1574/celestial audio CA 526

angela rost/marcelo alvarez/elena garanca/mihaela ungureanu/michael roider/martin müller/markus nieminen/peter koves/eijiro kai/wolfgang bankl/dan paul dimitrescu/janusz monarcha

302/18 october 2004/televised performance in wiener staatsoper
verdi don carlo/conductor bertrand de billy/*french version*
cd: orfeo C648 054/premiere 1708
dvd: tdk DVWW-OPCARLOS

ramon vargas/iano tamar/nadja michael/bo skovhus/alastair miles/simon yang/dan paul dimitrescu/cornelia salje/benedikt kobel/cosmin ifrim/inna los/Johannes gisser

303/30 october 2004/wiener staatsoper
beethoven fidelio/conductor seiji ozawa
cd: premiere 1716

waltraud meier/genia kühmeier/johan botha/cosmin ifrim/kurt rydl/falk struckmann/peter weber/alexander pinderak/friedrich springer

304/5 february 2005/concert performance in wiener staatsoper
bellini norma/conductor marcello viotti
cd: private edition vienna

edita gruberova/nadia krasteva/salvatore licitra/dan paul dimitrescu/ inna los/marian tabala

305/22 february 2005/televised performance in wiener staatsoper
massenet werther/conductor philippe Jordan
dvd: tdk DVWW-OPWER

marcelo alvarez/elina garanca/adrian eröd/alfred sramek/Ileana tonca/ peter jelosits/marcus pelz/gabriella bessenyei/clemens unterreiner

306/22 march 2005/wiener staatsoper
bellini i puritani/conductor frederic chaslin
cd: live rare opera/celestial audio CA 537

elena mosuc/juan diego florez/janusz monarcha/alastair miles/roberto frontali/benedikt kobel/antigone papoulkas

307/3 april 2005/televised performance in wiener staatsoper
donizetti l'elisir d'amore/conductor alfred eschwe
cd: live rare opera LRO 294/premiere 1812
dvd: virgin 363 3529

anna netrebko/rolando villazon/leo nucci/ildebrando d'arcangelo/inna los/konrad monsberger/michael burggasser

308/7 april 2005/wiener staatsoper
berg wozzeck/conductor seiji ozawa
cd: opera lovers 200501

franz hawlata/deborah polaski/wolfgang schmidt/benedikt kobel/michael roider/walter fink/Johannes wiedecke/hans peter kammerer/janina baechle/peter jelosits

309/26 may 2005/wiener staatsoper
rossini l'italiana in algeri/conductor frederic chaslin
cd: live rare opera LRO 297/opera lovers 200501

daniela barcellona/juan diego florez/wolfgang bankl/alfred sramek/bori keszei/hans peter kammerer/waltraud winsauer

310/4 june 2005/wiener staatsoper
puccini manon lescaut/conductor seiji ozawa
cd: premiere 1793

barbara haveman/neil shicoff/boaz daniel/wolfgang bankl/saimir pirgu/ marcus pelz/Johannes wiedecke

311/10 june 2005/wiener staatsoper
wagner parsifal/conductor christian thielemann
cd: private edition vienna/deutsche grammophon 477 6006

placido domingo/waltraud meier/franz Josef selig/falk struckmann/ wolfgang bankl/ain anger/benedikt kobel/in-sung kim/janina baechle/ daniela denschlag/john dickie/peter jelosits/inna loos/bori keszei/ antigone papoulkas/simian ivan/ildiko Raimondi/nadia krastea

312/3 december 2005/wiener staatsoper
wagner lohengrin/conductor semyon bychkov
cd: private edition vienna/house of opera HO 3566/
premiere 2099

Johan botha/soile isokoski/janina baechle/falk struckmann/kwangchul youn/adrian eröd

313/17 march 2006/wiener staatsoper
wagner lohengrin/conductor semyon bychkov
cd: premiere 2149

Johan botha/soile isokoski/janina baechle/falk struckmann/kwangchul youn/boaz Daniel

314/10 may 2006/wiener staatsoper
gounod romeo et juliette/conductor bertrand de billy
cd: private edition vienna

rolando villlazon/anna netrebko/michaela selinger/janina baechle/marian talaba/meng-chien ho/eijiro kai/hans peter kammerer/clemens unterreiner/in-sung kim/Johannes wiedecke/janusz monarcha

315/3 june 2006/televised performance in wiener staatsoper
schoenberg moses und aron/conductor daniele gatti
dvd: arthaus musik 101 259

franz grundheber/thomas moser/ildiko raimondi/janina baechle/
peter jelosits/morten frank larsen/georg tichy/alexandru moisuc/
johann reinprecht

316/16 september 2006/wiener staatsoper
donizetti roberto devereux/conductor friedrich haider
cd: celestial audio CA 603

joseph calleja/edita gruberova/sonia ganassi/roberto frontali/cosman ifrim/marcus pelz/Johannes gasser/hiro ijichi

317/23 september 2006/wiener staatsoper
verdi i vespri siciliani/conductor fabio luisi
cd: premiere 2374

sondra radvanovsky/francisco casanova/leo nucci/dan paul dimitrescu/clemens unterreiner/roberto scandiuzzi/daniela denschlag/marian talaba/peter jelosits/eijiro kai

318/25 october 2006/wiener staatsoper
verdi otello/conductor daniele gatti
cd: opera lovers 200601

Johan botha/falk struckmann/krassimira stoyanova/nadia krasteva/marian talaba/cosmin ifrim/ain anger/vladimir moroz/hacik bayvertian

319/19 november 2006/wiener staatsoper
bellini la sonnambula/conductor pier giorgio morandi
cd: opera lovers 200601

anna netrebko/antonino siragusa/michele pertusi/janina baechle/simian ivan/Marcus pelz/johann reinprecht

320/3 march 2007/wiener staatsoper
massenet manon/conductor bertrand de billy
cd: premiere 2591/private edition vienna

anna neterbko/roberto alagna/ain anger/adrian eröd/michael roider/in-sung kim/simian ivan/sophie marilley/Juliette mars/elisabeth van der vloedt/ hans peter kammerer/jacek krzyszkowski

321/1 april 2007/televised performance in wiener staatsoper
donizetti la fille du regiment/conductor yves abel
cd: live rare opera
dvd: encore 2871

natalie dessay/juan diego florez/janina baechle/montserrat caballe/carlos alvarez/clemens unterreiner/konrad Huber/wolfram igor derntl/ carlos chies

322/28 october 2007/wiener staatsoper
tchaikovsky pique dame/conductor seiji ozawa
cd: premiere 2773

neil shicoff/martina serafin/anja silja/albert dohmen/markus eiche/peter jelosits/goran simic/benedikt kobel/dan paul dimitrescu/clemens unterreiner/nadia krasteva/

323/16 december 2007/wiener staatsoper
wagner die walküre/conductor franz welser-möst
cd: private edition vienna

eva Johansson/nina stemme/michaela schuster/johan botha/juha uusitalo/ waller fink/manda mace/caroline wenborne/alexandra reinprecht/aura twarowska/sophie marilley/cornelia salje/Daniela denschlag/ zoyana kushpler

324/8 january 2008/wiener staatsoper
massenet werther/conductor marco armiliato
cd: premiere 2887

rolando villazon/sophie koch/markus eiche/laura tatulescu/alfred sramek/ peter jelosits/marcus pelz

325/12 january 2008/wiener staatsoper
wagner die meistersinger von nürnberg/conductor
christian thielemann
cd: private edition vienna

falk struckmann/ain anger/peter seiffert/norbert ernst/ricarda merbeth/
michaela selinger/adrian eröd/alexander kaimbacher/marcus pelz/
wolfgang koch/cosmin ifrim/michael roider/peter jelosits/clemens
unterreiner/alfred sramek/janusz monarcha/wolfgang bankl

326/19-23 january 2008/televised performances in wiener staatsoper
wagner die meistersinger von nürnberg/conductor
christian thielemann
dvd: euroarts 207 2488

falk struckmann/ain anger/johan botha/norbert rrnst/ricarda merbeth/
michaela schuster/adrian eröd/alexander kaimbacher/marcus pelz/
wolfgang koch/cosmin ifrim/michael roider/peter jelosits/cjemens
unterreiner/alfred sramek/janusz monarcha/wolfgang bankl

327/1 march 2008/wiener staatsoper
verdi la forza del destino/conductor zubin mehta
cd: opera lovers 200801

nina stemme/nadia krasteva/carlos alvarez/alastair miles/salvatore licitra/
elisabeta marin/tiziano bracci/dan paul dimitrescu/michael roider/
clemens unterreiner

328/27 april 2008/wiener staatsoper
wagner siegfried/conductor franz welser-möst
cd: private edition vienna

stephen gould/juha uusitalo/nina stemme/anna larsson/tomasz konieczny/
herwig pecoraro/ain anger/Ileana tonca

329/8 december 2008/wiener staatsoper
wagner götterdämmerung/conductor franz welser-möst
cd: private edition vienna

eva Johansson/caroline wenborne/miholo fujimura/Stephen gould/boaz
daniel/ric halfvarson/tomasz konieczny/zoyrana/elisabeth kulman/
Ileana tonca/michaela selinger/Juliette mars

330/7 march 2009/wiener staatsoper
tchaikovsky evgeny onegin/conductor seiji ozawa
cd: private edition vienna

simon keenlyside/ramon vargas/tamar iveri/nadia krasteva/aura twarowska/
margareta hintermeier/ain anger/ans peter kammerer/marcus pelz/
alexander kaimbacher/wolfram igor derntl

331/2 may 2009/wiener staatsoper
wagner das rheingold/conductor franz welser-möst
cd: private edition vienna

juha uusitalo/janina baechle/ricarda merbeth/markus eiche/gergely nemeti/
adrian eröd/tomasz konieczny/herwig pecoraro/sorin coliban/ain anger/
anna larsson/Ileana tonca/michaela selinger/elisabeth kulman

332/8 january 2010/wiener staatsoper
massenet manon/conductor bertrand de billy
cd: private edition vienna

diana damrau/ramon vargas/markus eiche/dan paul dimitrescu/alexander
kaimbacher/clemens unterreiner/simian ivan/sophie marilley/zoryana
kushpler/renate gutsch/hacik bayvertian

333/5 april 2011/televised performance in wiener staatsoper
donizetti anna bolena/conductor evelino pido
dvd: deutsche grammophon 073 4725

anna netrebko/elena garanca/ildebrando d'arcangelo/francesco meli/
elisabeth kulman/dan paul dimitrescu/peter jelosits

334/1 november 2011/wiener staatsoper
wagner das rheingold/conductor christian thielemann
cd: deutsche grammophon 479 1560

albert dohmen/markus eiche/herbert lippert/adrian eröd/tomasz
konieczny/wolfgang schmidt/lars woldt/ain anger/janina baechle/
alexandra reinprecht/anna larsson/ileana tonca/ulrike helzel/
zoryana kushpler

335/6 november 2011/wiener staatsoper
wagner die walküre/conductor christian thielemann
cd: deutsche grammophon 479 1560

katarina dalayman/waltraud meier/janina baechle/albert dohmen/christopher ventris/eric halfvarson/ildiko raimondi/alexandra reinprecht/aura twarowska/ zoryana kushpler/donna ellen/ulrike helzel/monica bohinec/Juliette mars

336/9 november 2011/wiener staatsoper
wagner siegfried/conductor christian thielemann
cd: deutsche grammophon 479 1560

stephen gould/linda watson/albert dohmen/wolfgang schmidt/tomasz konieczny/ain anger/anna larsson/chen reiss

337/13 november 2011/wiener staatsoper
wagner götterdämmerung/conductor christian thielemann
cd: deutsche grammophon 479 1560

linda watson/stephen gould/attila jun/markus eiche/tomasz konieczny/caroline wenborne/janina baechle/zoryana kushpler/ulrike helzel/ildiko raimondi/ ileana tonca

337a/19 december 2012/wiener staatsoper
strauss ariadne auf naxos/conductor franz welser-möst
cd: private edition vienna

krassimira stoyanova/christine schäfer/daniela fally/stephen gould/adam piachetka/ carlos osuna/andreas hörl/pavel kolgatin/jochen schmeckenbacher/norbert ernst/ marcus pelz/daniel lökös/peter matic/valentina nafornita/margarita gritskova/ olga bezsmertna

338/15 april 2013/wiener staatsoper
tchaikovsky evgeny onegin/conductor andris nelsons
cd: private edition vienna

dmitri hvorostovsky/dmitry korchak/anna netrebko/alias kolosova/konstantin gorny/zoyana kushpler/mihail dogotari/norbert ernst

339/5 october 2013/televised performance in wiener staatsoper
puccini la fanciulla del west/conductor franz welser-möst
dvd: sony classical 88875 064069/88875 064079

nina stemme/jonas kaufmann/tomasz konieczny/norbert ernst/paolo rumetz/ boaz daniel/michael roider/hans peter kammerer/tao-joong yang/peter jelosits/carlos osuna/clemens unterreiner/il hong/jongmin park/Juliette mars/alessio arduini/wolfram igor drntl

340/21 june 2014/wiener staatsoper
janacek the cunning little vixen/conductor franz welser-möst
cd: private edition vienna

chen reiss/gerald finley/donna ellen/andreas hörl/wolfgang bankl/wolfram igor derntl/sabine kogler/jan sebastian höhener/bernhard sengstschmid/ isolde zerweck/hyuna ko/james kryshak/heinz zednik

341/15 november 2014/wiener staatsoper
mussorgsky khovantschina/conductor semyon bychkov
cd: private edition vienna

ferruccio furlanetto/christopher ventris/elena maxinov/herbert lippert/andrzej dobber/ain anger/lydia rathkolb/caroline wenborne/marcus pelz/marian talaba/wolfram igor derntl/hans peter kammerer/il hong/benedikt kobel/nornert ernst

342/4 april 2015/wiener staatsoper
strauss elektra/conductor mikko franck
cd: private edition vienna

nina stemme/ricarda merbeth/anna larsson/norbert ernst/falk struckmann/donna ellen/monica bohinec/juliette mars/ulrike helzel/regine hansler/ildiko raimondi/thomas ebenstein/marcus pelz/aura twarkowska/janusz monarcha

343/30 may 2015/wiener staatsoper
wagner das rheingold/conductor simon rattle
cd: private edition vienna

tomasz konieczny/boaz daniel/jason bridges/herbert lippert/michaela schuster/
olga bezsmertna/janina baechle/richard paul fink/herwig pecoraro/peter rose/
mikhail petrenko/Ileana tonca/ulrike helzel/Juliette mars

344/31 may 2015/wiener staatsoper
wagner die walküre/conductor simon rattle
cd: private edition vienna

evelyn herlitzius/martina serafin/michaela schuster/christopher ventris/tomasz
konieczny/mikhail petrenko/donna ellen/ildiko raimondi/huyana ko/
margaret plummer/ulrike helzel/monica bohinec/carole wilson/Juliette mars

345/4 june 2015/wiener staatsoper
wagner siegfried/conductor simon rattle
cd: private edition vienna

stephen gould/evelyn herlitzius/tomasz konieczny/herwig pecoraro/richard
paul fink/mikhail petrenko/janina baechle/annika gerhards

346/7 june 2015/wiener staatsoper
wagner götterdämmerung/conductor simon rattle
cd: private edition vienna

evelyn herlitzius/stephen gould/falk struckmann/caroline wenborne/boaz daniel/richard paul fink/anne sofie von otter/monica bohinec/stephanie houtzeel/ildiko raimondi/Ileana tonca/ulrike helzel/Juliette mars

347/19 november 2015/wiener staatsoper
humperdinck hänsel und gretel/conductor christian thielemann
cd: private edition vienna

ileana tonca/daniela sindram/janina baechle/clemens unterreiner/
michaela schuster/annika gerhards

348/15 december 2015/wiener staatsoper
janacek vec makropulos/conductor jakub hrusa
cd: premiere

laura aikin/ludovit ludha/thomas eberstein/margarita gritskova/markus marquardt/carlos osuna/wolfgang bankl/marcus pelz/aura twarowska/ heinz zednik/ilseyar khayrullova

PART FOUR: COMPLETE BROADCASTS WHICH REMAIN UNPUBLISHED

18 august 1941 (salzburg)
mozart don giovanni/conductor hans knappertsbusch

14-16 november 1944
mozart die zauberflöte/conductor karl böhm

27 september 1947 (london)
mozart don giovanni/conductor josef krips

21 october 1950
tchaikovsky evgeny onegin/conductor meinhard von zallinger

8 april 1956
strauss elektra/conductor karl böhm

19 october 1956
wagner tannhäuser/conductor rudolf moralt

16 february 1963
gounod faust/conductor georges pretre

21 june 1964
strauss arabella/conductor joseph keilberth

17 april 1965
strauss daphne/conductor karl böhm

28 march 1966
puccini la boheme/conductor leopold hager

unpublished broadcasts/continued

20 june 1966
mozart le nozze di figaro/conductor josef krips

16 october 1966
offenbach les contes d'hoffmann/conductor josef krips

28 april 1967
mozart le nozze di figaro/conductor karl böhm

15 june 1967
mozart don giovanni/conductor josef krips

9 november 1967
von einem dantons tod/conductor josef krips

2 may 1969
strauss arabella/conductor berislav klobucar

15 december 1971
mozart die zauberflöte/conductor Josef krips

21 april 1972
puccini madama butterfly/conductor berislav klobucar

21 june 1972
strauss der rosenkavalier/conductor heinz wallberg

unpublished broadcasts/continued

12 october 1972
mozart don giovanni/conductor Josef krips

4 september 1975
strauss elektra/conductor karl böhm

17 december 1976
von einem kabale und liebe/christoph von dohnanyi

10 february 1977
puccini madama butterfly/conductor berislav klobucar

28 may 1978
puccini tosca/alberto erede

2 october 1978
strauss der rosenkavalier/conductor reinhard schwarz

15 january 1980
verdi rigoletto/conductor miguel gomez-martinez

23 january 1981 (concert performance)
halevy la juive/conductor gerd albrecht

12 march 1981
mozart le nozze di figaro/conductor karl böhm

22 october 1981
rossini la cenerentola/conductor roberto abbado

unpublished broadcasts/continued

24 january 1982
strauss ariadne auf naxos/conductor wilfried böttcher

12 september 1982
verdi otello/conductor adam fischer

20 november 1982
strauss der rosenkavalier/conductor horst stein

22 november 1982
tchaikovsky pique dame/conductor dimitri kitaenko

13 february 1983 (concert performance)
wagner die feen/conductor sixten ehrling

4 march 1984
verdi la traviata/conductor anton guadagno

20 april 1984
verdi aida/conductor lorin maazel

25 april 1984
donizetti l'elisir d'amore/conductor niksa bareza

9 june 1985
wagner die walküre/conductor peter schneider

unpublished broadcasts/continued

10 february 1986
puccini tosca/conductor anton guadagno

19 october 1986
verdi un ballo in maschera/conductor claudio abbado

17 march 1987
mozart cosi fan tutte/conductor adam fischer

19 march 1988
mozart die zauberflöte/conductor nikolaus harnoncourt

23 february 1992
strauss die frau ohne schatten/conductor horst stein

8 may 1993
verdi la forza del destino/conductor marcello viotti

29 may 1993
verdi aida/conductor christian badea

17 april 1995
giordano fedora/conductor fabio luisi

3 february 1996
wagner der fliegende holländer/conductor simone young

26 february 1996
verdi il trovatore/conductor stefan soltesz

4 march 1999
rossini il barbiere di siviglia/conductor jan latham Koenig

unpublished broadcasts/continued

11 march 2000
mascagni cavalleria rusticana/leoncavallo i pagliacci/
conductor arthur fagen

29 may 2000
rossini il barbiere di siviglia/conductor ralf weikert

2 october 2000
puccini gianni schicchi/conductor michael boder

25 december 2000
strauss die frau ohne schatten/conductor simone young

1 october 2002
britten billy budd/conductor richard hickox

18 november 2002
strauss die frau ohne schatten/conductor michael boder

6 september 2003
verdi simon boccanegra/conductor daniele gatti

24 october 2003
strauss die frau ohne schatten/conductr peter schneider

12 june 2006
mozart die zauberflöte/conductor michael halasz

unpublished broadcasts/concluded

5 january 2007
mozart le nozze di figaro/conductor philippe Jordan

27 june 2007
verdi la traviata/conductor roberto palumbo

26 may 2009
tchaikovsky evgeny onegin/conductor seiji ozawa

17 october 2010
hindemith cardillac/conductor franz welser-möst

PART FIVE: INDEX OF OPERAS
session number and conductor

ludwig van beethoven/**fidelio**
012/karl böhm
017/clemens krauss
020/wilhelm furtwängler
026/karl böhm
044/herbert von karajan
056/herbert von karajan
101/leonard bernstein
159/leonard bernstein
303/seiji ozawa

vincenzo bellini/**norma**
151/riccardo muti
304/marcello viotti

i puritani
236/placido domingo
298/stefan soltesz
306/frederic chaslin

la sonnambula
276/stefano renzani
319/pier giorgio morandi

148

alban berg/**lulu**
094/karl böhm
194/lorin maazel

wozzeck
032/karl böhm
062/leopold ludwig
308/seiji ozawa

hector berlioz/**les troyens**
144/gerd Albrecht

georges bizet/**carmen**
052/herbert von karajan
079/lorin maazel
167/carlos kleiber
196/lorin maazel
240/donald runnicles
275/vjekoslav sutej

alexander borodin/**prince igor**
037/lovro von matacic

benjamin britten/**billy budd**
271/donald runnicles

149
friedrich cerha/**der riese vom steinfeld**
285/michael boder

luigi cherubini/**medea**
118/horst stein

claude debussy/**pelleas et melisande**
053/herbert von karajan
083/andre cluytens

gaetono donizetti/**anna bolena**
333/evelino pido

don pasquale
152/hector urbon

l'elisir d'amore
307/alfred eschew

la favorite
259/fabio luisi
297/vjekoslav sutej

la fille du regiment
321/yves abel

lucia di lammermoor
161/giuseppe patane
163/giuseppe patane
164/giuseppe patane
184/hans graf
284/frederic chaslin

150
donizetti/**roberto devereux**
286/frederic chaslin
316/friedrich haider

antonin dvorak/**rusalka**
204/vaclav neumann

gottfried von einem/**der besuch der alten dame**
112/horst stein

george enescu/**oedipe**
247/michael gielen

umberto giordano/**andrea chenier**
024/rudolf moralt
040/lovro von matacic
180/nello santi
189/riccardo chailly
228/marcello viotti
237/marcello viotti
293/adam fischer

fedora
238/fabio luisi
261/anton guadagno
294/stefano ranzani

151

charles gounod/**faust**
092/ernst märzendorfer
127/ernst märzendorfer
200/erich binder

romeo et juliette
282/marcello viotti
288/marcello viotti
301/marcello viotti
314/bertrand de billy

jacques fromental halevy/**la juive**
262/simone young
290/vjekoslav sutej

engelbert humperdinck/**hänsel und gretel**
347/christian thielemann

leos janacek/**the cunning little vixen**
340/franz welser-möst

jenufa
066/jaroslav krombholc
122/janos kulka
280/seiji ozawa

the makropoulos case
348/jakub hrusa

152

ruggero leoncavallo/**i pagliacci**
097/berislav klobucar
201/adam fischer
231/michael halasz
279/adam fischer

albert lortzing/**der wildschütz**
042/heinz wallberg

pietro mascagni/**cavalleria rusticana**
232/michael halasz

jules massenet/**herodiade**
241/marcello viotti

manon
116/serge baudo
195/adam fischer
320/bertrand de billy
332/bertrand de billy

werther
305/philippe Jordan
324/marco armiliato

saverio mercadante/**il giuramento**
172/gerd albrecht

153
giacomo meyerbeer/**le prophete**
252/marcello viotti

claudio monteverdi/**l'incoronazione di poppea**
060/herbert von karajan

wolfgang amadeus mozart/**cosi fan tutte**
078/karl böhm
093/Josef krips
283/riccardo muti

don giovanni
002/bruno walter
022/karl böhm
027/karl böhm
058/joseph keilberth
064/herbert von karajan
134/leopold hager
260/riccardo muti

idomeneo
108/jaroslav krombholc

mozart/**le nozze di figaro**
004/bruno walter
007/hans knappertsbusch
009/clemens krauss
154/herbert von karajan
178/karl böhm
222/claudio abbado
251/jun märkl
273/riccardo muti

die zauberflöte
001/arturo toscanini
008/karl böhm
057/herbert von karajan

modest mussorgsky/**khovantschina**
214/claudio abbado
218/claudio abbado
341/semyon bychkov

jacques offenbach/**les contes d'hoffmann**
233/christian badea

155

hans pfitzner/**palestrina**
073/robert heger
099/hans swarowsky

Ildebrando pizzetti/**assassino nella cattedrale**
038/herbert von karajan

amilcare ponchielli/**la gioconda**
202/adam fischer

francis poulenc/**dialogues des carmelites**
051/berislav klobucar

giacomo puccini/**la boheme**
065/herbert von karajan
130/anton guadagno
155/herbert von karajan
263/jun märkl

madama butterfly
047/berislav klobucar

la fanciulla del west
169/giuseppe patane
339/franz welser-möst

il trittico
168/gerd albrecht

156

puccini/**manon lescaut**
072/mario rossi
234/antonio pappano
310/seiji ozawa

tosca
054/herbert von karajan
082/andre cluytens
087/josef krips
100/berislav klobucar
148/horst stein
149/horst stein
150/alberto erede
210/garcia navarro
265/vjekoslav sutej

turandot
034/mario rossi
049/francesco molinari-pradelli
126/berislav klobucar
191/lorin maazel
192/lorin maazel

157
gioachino rossini/**il barbiere di siviglia**
080/karl böhm
166/carlo felice cillario

la cenerentola
036/alberto erede
181/roberto abbado

guillaume tell
255/fabio luisi

l'italiana in algeri
209/claudio abbado
239/marcello viotti
309/frederic chaslin

arnold schoenberg/**moses und aaron**
315/daniele gatti

dimitri shostakovich/**katerina ismailova**
074/jaroslav krombholc

bedrich smetana/**the bartered bride**
043/berislav klobucar
182/adam fischer

dalibor
096/josef krips

158

johann strauss/**die fledermaus**
045/herbert von karajan
173/theodor guschlbauer

richard strauss/**die ägyptische helena**
106/Josef krips

arabella
010/clemens krauss

ariadne auf naxos
014/karl böhm
088/karl böhm
089/karl böhm
146/karl böhm
253/peter Schneider
337a/franz welser-möst

capriccio
039/karl böhm
067/georges pretre
190/heinrich hollreiser

daphne
013/karl böhm
300/semyon bychkov

159

strauss/**elektra**
077/karl böhm
156/horst stein
217/claudio abbado
342/mikko franck

die frau ohne schatten
028/karl böhm
068/herbert von karajan
069/herbert von karajan
157/karl böhm
198/christoph von dohnanyi
264/giuseppe sinopoli
266/giuseppe sinopoli

friedenstag
006/clemens krauss

intermezzo
021/rudolf moralt
061/joseph keilberth

160

strauss/**der rosenkavalier**
031/hans knappertsbusch
090/leonard bernstein
115/josef krips
165/reinhold schwarz
235/carlos kleiber

salome
018/clemens krauss
076/zdenek kosler
123/karl böhm
225/peter scneider

piotr tchaikovsky/**evgeny onegin**
025/berislav klobucar
046/lovro von matacic
212/seiji ozawa
330/seiji ozawa
338/andris nelsons

pique dame
258/seiji ozawa
322/seiji ozawa

161
giuseppe verdi/**aida**
029/rafael kubrlik
063/lovro von matacic
070/herbert von karajan
124/riccardo muti
242/placido domingo
248/marcello viotti
270/fabio luisi

attila
179/giuseppe sinopoli

un ballo in maschera
109/berislav klobucar
113/silvio varviso
128/anton guadagno
145/giuseppe patane
158/miguel gomez martinez
203/claudio abbado
207/claudio abbado

162
verdi/**don carlo**
050/nello santi
084/berislav klobucar
085/berislav klobucar
088/berislav klobucar
091/silvio varviso
105/horst stein
120/silvio varviso
138/anton guadagno
142/miguel gomez martinez
171/herbert von karajan
219/claudio abbado
281/leopold hager

don carlos/*french version*
302/bertrand de billy

ernani
256/seiji ozawa
259/seiji ozawa

163
verdi/**falstaff**
005/arturo toscanini
175/georg solti
187/lorin maazel
230/seiji ozawa

la forza del destino
041/dimitri mitropoulos
136/riccardo muti
176/miguel gomez martinez
327/zubin mehta

luisa miller
132/alberto erede

macbeth
011/karl böhm
098/karl böhm
103/berislav klobucar

nabucco
272/fabio luisi

164

verdi/**otello**

015/karl böhm
111/heinz wallberg
135/alberto erede
137/heinz wallberg
141/heinz wallberg
183/james levine
205/zubin mehta
206/zubin mehta
208/adam fischer
211/adam fischer
215/adam fischer
216/adam fischer
223/michael schonwandt
224/berislav klobucar
227/jan latham-koenig
243/christian badea
244/donald runnicles
245/michael halasz
245/daniel oren
246/marcello viotti
249/adam fischer
269/marcello viotti
278/marcello viotti
318/daniele gatti

165
verdi/**rigoletto**
055/tullio serafin
104/carlo franci
121/heinz wallberg
125/georges singer
133/walter weller
160/giuseppe patane
188/riccardo muti
254/michael halasz

simon boccanegra
095/josef krips
197/claudio abbado
287/daniele gatti

la traviata
073/berislav klobucar
117/josef krips
174/alberto erede
177/gianfranco masini
185/nello santi
226/jan latham-koenig

166

verdi/**il trovatore**
081/argeo quadri
110/horst stein
131/anton guadagno
140/ralf weikert
153/herbert von karajan
162/herbert von karajan
193/charles mackerras
268/arthur fagen

I vespri siciliani
274/anton guadagno
317/fabio luisi

richard wagner/**götterdämmerung**
329/franz welser-möst
337/christian thielemann
347/simon rattle

der fliegende holländer
019/rudolf moralt
295/seiji ozawa
296/seiji ozawa

167

wagner/**lohengrin**
075/karl böhm
199/peter schneider
220/claudio abbado
312/semyon bychkov
313/semyon bychkov

die meistersinger von nürnberg
003/arturo toscanini
016/karl böhm
023/karl böhm
030/fritz reiner
139/christoph von dohnanyi
221/colin davis
325/christian thielemann
326/christian thielemann

parsifal
048/herbert von karajan
107/charles vanderzand
170/horst stein
257/jun märkl
299/donald runnicles
311/christian thielemann

168
wagner/**das rheingold**
143/horst stein
331/franz welser-möst
334/christian thielemann
343/simon rattle

rienzi
250/zubin mehta

siegfried
328/franz welser-möst
336/christian thielemann
345/simon rattle

tannhäuser
059/herbert von karajan
114/berislav klobucar
186/lorin maazel
213/giuseppe sinopoli

wagner/**tristan und isolde**
033/andre cluytens
102/horst stein
129/carlos kleiber
147/horst stein
267/semyon bychkov
291/christian thielemann
292/christian thielemann

die walküre
035/herbert von karajan
229/christoph von dohnanyi
277/peter schneider
323/franz welser-möst
335/christian thielemann
344/simon rattle

carl maria von weber/**der freischütz**
119/karl böhm

PART SIX: INDEX OF CONDUCTORS

yves abel
321/la fille du regiment

marco armiliato
324/werther

claudio abbado/1933-2014
197/simon boccanegra
203/un ballo in maschera
207/un ballo in maschera
209/l'italiana in algeri
214/khovantschina
217/elektra
218/khovantschina
219/don carlo
220/lohengrin
222/le nozze di Figaro

roberto abbado/born 1954
181/la cenerentola

gerd albrecht/1935-2014
144/les troyens
168/il trittico
172/il giuramento

christian badea
233/les contes d'hoffmann
243/otello

serge baudo/born 1927
116/manon

leonard bernstein/1918-1990
090/der rosenkavalier
101/fidelio
159/fidelio

bertrand de billy/born 1965
302/don carlos (french version)
314/romeo et Juliette
320/manon
332/manon

erich binder/born 1947
200/faust

michael boder/born 1958
285/der riese vom steinfeld

karl böhm/1894-1981
008/die zauberflöte
011/macbeth
012/fidelio
013/daphne
014/ariadne auf naxos
015/otello
016/die meistersinger von nürnberg
022/don giovanni
023/die meistersinger von nürnberg
026/fidelio
027/don giovanni
028/die frau ohne schatten
032/wozzeck
039/capriccio
075/lohengrin
077/elektra
078/cosi fan tutte
080/il barbiere di siviglia
088/ariadne auf naxos
089/ariadne auf naxos
094/lulu
098/macbeth
119/der freischütz
123/salome
146/ariadne auf naxos
157/die frau ohne schatten
178/le nozze di figaro

semyon bychkov/born 1952
267/tristan und isolde
300/daphne
312/lohengrin
313/lohengrin
341/khovantschina

riccardo chailly/born 1953
189/andrea chenier

frederic chaslin/born 1963
284/lucia di lammermoor
286/roberto devereux
306/i puritan
309/l'italiana in algeri

carlo felice cillario/1915-2007
166/il barbiere di siviglia

andre cluytens/1905-1967
053/tristan und isolde
082/tosca
083/pelleas et melisande

colin davis/1927-2013
221/die meistersinger von nürnberg

175

christoph von dohnanyi/born 1929
139/die meistersinger von nürnberg
198/die frau ohne schatten
229/die walküre

placido domingo/born 1941
236/i puritan
242/aida

alberto erede/1908-2001
036/la cenerentola
132/luisa miller
135/otello
150/tosca
174/la traviata

alfred eschwe/born 1949
307/l'elisir d'amore

arthur fagen/born 1951
268/il trovatore

176
adam fischer/born 1949
182/the bartered bride
195/manon
201/ i pagliacci
202/la gioconda
208/otello
211/otello
215/otello
216/otello
249/otello
279/i pagliacci
293/andrea chenier

carlo franci/born 1927
104/rigoletto

mikko franck/born 1979
342/elektra

wilhelm furtwängler/1886-1954
020/fidelio

daniele gatti/born 1961
287/simon boccanegra
315/moses und aron
318/otello

michael gielen/born 1927
247/oedipe

miguel gomez martinez/born 1949
142/don carlo
158/un ballo in maschera
176/la forza del destino

hans graf/born 1949
184/lucia di lammermoor

anton guadagno/1925-2002
128/un ballo in maschera
130/la boheme
131/il trovatore
138/don carlo
274/i vespri siciliani
261/fedora

theodor guschlbauer/born 1939
173/die fledermaus

leopold hager/born 1935
104/don giovanni
281/don carlo

friedrich haider/born 1961
316/roberto devereux

michael halasz/born 1938
231/i pagliacci
232/cavalleria rusticana
245/otello
254/rigoletto

robert heger/1886-1978
073/palestrina

heinrich hollreiser/1913-2006
190/capriccio

jakub hrusa/born 1981
348/makropoulos case

philippe jordan/born 1974
305/werther

herbert von karajan/1908-1989
035/die walküre
038/assassino nella cattedrale
044/fidelio
045/die fledermaus
048/parsifal
052/carmen
053/pelleas et melisande
054/tosca
056/fidelio
057/die zauberflöte
059/tannhäuser
060/l'incoronazione di poppea
064/don giovanni
065/la boheme
068/die frau ohne schatten
069/die frau ohne schatten
070/aida
153/il trovatore
154/le nozze di figaro
162/il trovatore
171/don carlo

joseph keilberth/1908-1968
058/don giovanni
061/intermezzo

carlos kleiber/1930-2004
129/tristan und isolde
167/carmen
235/der rosenkavalier

berislav klobucar/1924-2014
025/evgeny onegin
043/the bartered bride
047/madama butterfly
051/dialogues des carmelites
073/la traviata
084/don carlo
085/don carlo
088/don carlo
097/i pagliacci
100/tosca
103/macbeth
109/un ballo in maschera
114/tannhäuser
126/turandot
224/otello

hans knappertsbusch/1888-1965
007/le nozze di figaro
031/der rosenkavalier

zdenek kosler/1928-1995
076/salome

clemens krauss/1893-1954
006/friedenstag
009/le nozze di figaro
010/arabella
017/fidelio
018/salome

josef krips/1902-1974
087/tosca
093/cosi fan tutte
095/simon boccanegra
096/dalibor
106/die ägyptische helena
115/der rosenkavalier
117/la traviata

jaroslav krombholc/1918-1983
066/jenufa
074/katerina ismailova
108/idomeneo

rafael kubelik/1914-1996
029/aida

janos kulka/1929-2001
122/jenufa

jan latham-koenig/born 1953
226/la traviata
227/otello

james levine/born 1943
183/otello

leopold ludwig/1908-1979
062/wozzeck

fabio luisi/born 1959
238/fedora
255/guillaume tell
270/aida
272/nabucco
289/la favorite
317/i vespri siciliani

183

lorin maazel/1930-2014
079/carmen
186/tannhäuser
187/falstaff
191/turandot
192/turandot
194/lulu
196/carmen

charles mackerras/1925-2010
193/il trovatore

jun märkl/born 1959
251/le nozze di figaro
257/parsifal
263/la boheme

ernst märzendorfer/1921-2009
092/faust
127/faust

gianfranco masini/1937-1993
177/la traviata

lovro von matacic/1899-1985
037/prince igor
040/andrea chenier
046/evgeny onegin
063/aida

zubin mehta/born 1936
205/otello
206/otello
250/rienzi
327/la forza del destino

dimitri mitropoulos/1896-1960
041/la forza del destino

francesco molinari-pradelli/1911-1996
049/turandot

rudolf moralt/1902-1958
019/der fliegende holländer
021/intermezzo
024/andrea chenier

pier giorgio morandi
319/i puritan

riccardo muti/born 1941
124/aida
136/la forza del destino
151/norma
188/rigoletto
260/don giovanni
273/le nozze di figaro
283/cosi fan tutte

185
garcia navarro/1941-2001
210/tosca

andris nelsons/born 1978
338/evgeny onegin

vaclav neumann/1920-1995
204/rusalka

daniel oren/born 1955
245/otello

seiji ozawa/born 1935
212/evgeny onegin
230/falstaff
256/ernani
258/pique dame
259/ernani
280/jenufa
295/der fliegende holländer
296/der fliegende holländer
303/fidelio
308/wozzeck
310/manon
322/pique dame
330/evgeny onegin

antonio pappano/born 1959
234/manon lescaut

giuseppe patane/1932-1989
145/un ballo in maschera
160/rigoletto
161/lucia di lammermoor
163/lucia di lammermoor
164/lucia di lammermoor
169/la fanciulla del west

evelino pido/born 1953
333/anna bolena

georges pretre/born 1924
067/capriccio

argeo quadri/1911-2004
081/il trovatore

stefano ranzani
276/la sonnambula
294/fedora

simon rattle/born 1955
343/das rheingold
344/die walküre
345/siegfried
347/götterdämmerung

fritz reiner/1888-1963
030/die meistersinger von nürnberg

mario rossi/1902-1992
034/turandot
072/manon lescaut

donald runnicles/born 1954
240/carmen
244/otello
271/billy budd
299/Parsifal

nello santi/born 1931
050/don carlo
180/andrea chenier
185/la traviata

peter schneider/born 1940
199/lohengrin
225/salome
253/ariadne auf naxos
277/die walküre

michael schonwandt/born 1953
223/otello

reinhard schwarz/1936-2005
165/der rosenkavalier

tullio serafin/1878-1968
055/rigoletto

georges singer/1908-1980
125/rigoletto

giuseppe sinopoli/1946-2001
179/attila
213/tannhäuser
264/die frau ohne schatten
266/die frau ohne schatten

stefan soltesz/born 1949
298/i puritani

georg solti/1912-1997
175/falstaff

189

horst stein/1928-2008
102/tristan und isolde
105/don carlo
110/il trovatore
112/der besuch der alten dame
118/medea
143/das rheingold
147/tristan und isolde
148/tosca
149/tosca
156/elektra
170/parsifal

vjekoslav sutej/1961-2009
265/tosca
275/carmen
290/la juive
297/la favourite

hans swarowsky/1899-1975
099/palestrina

christian thielemann/born 1959
291/tristan und isolde
292/tristan und isolde
311/parsifal
325/die meistersinger von nürnberg
326/die meistersinger von nürnberg
334/das rheingold
335/die walküre
336/siegfried
337/götterdämmerung
347/hänsel und gretel

arturo toscanini/1867-1957
001/die zauberflöte
003/die meistersinger von nürnberg
005/falstaff

hector urbon
152/don pasquale

charles vanderzand
107/parsifal

silvio varviso/1924-2006
091/don carlo
113/un ballo in maschera
120/don carlo

marcello viotti/1954-2005
228/andrea chenier
237/andrea chenier
239/l'italiana in algeri
241/herodiade
246/otello
248/aida
252/le prophete
269/otello
278/otello
282/romeo et juliette
288/romeo et juliette
301/romeo et juliette
304/norma

heinz wallberg/1923-2004
042/der wildschütz
111/otello
121/rigoletto
137/otello
141/otello

bruno walter/1876-1962
002/don giovanni
004/le nozze di figaro

ralf weikert/born 1940
140/il trovatore

walter weller/1939-2015
133/rigoletto

franz welser-möst/born 1960
323/die walküre
328/siegfried
329/götterdämmerung
331/das rheingold
337a/ariadne auf naxos
339/la fanciulla del west
340/the cunning little vixen

simone young/born 1961
262/la juive

PART SEVEN: A PERSONAL COLLECTION
performances attended at the vienna staatsoper by john hunt

1 september 1965
le nozze di figaro/conductor Josef krips

28 march 1967
un ballo in maschera/conductor heinz wallberg

29 march 1967
fidelio/conductor karl böhm

30 march 1967
madama butterfly/conductor heinz wallberg

31 march 1967
the bartered bride/conductor berislav klobucar

29 march 1969
la boheme/conductor wilhelm loibner

30 march 1969
die walküre/conductor hans wallat

5 april 1969
la boheme/conductor wilhelm loibner

6 april 1969
parsifal/conductor robert heger

26 march 1970
parsifal/conductor robert heger

30 march 1972
la boheme/conductor silvio varviso

11 april 1974
medea/conductor alexander sander

1 april 1975
aida/conductor leopold hager

1 april 1977
norma/conductor riccardo muti

3 april 1977
salome/conductor gerd albrecht

4 april 1977
norma/conductor riccardo muti

5 april 1977
parsifal/conductor günther wich

14 april 1982
la boheme/conductor ernst märzendorfer

24 march 1983
rigoletto/conductor riccardo muti

25 march 1983
die entführung aus dem serail/conductor theodor guschlbauer

195

15 april 1984
parsifal/conductor horst stein

16 april 1984
andrea chenier/conductor anton guadagno

17 april 1984
ariadne auf naxos/conductor christof prick

18 april 1984
l'elisir d'amore/conductor niksa bareza

23 march 1985
faust/conductor erich binder

24 march 1985
pique dame/conductor dimitri kitaenko

1 april 1985
die frau ohne schatten/conductor horst stein

9 april 1987
macbeth/conductor charles mackerras

10 april 1987
rusalka/conductor vaclav neumann

6 april 1988
die zauberflöte/conductor nikolaus harnoncourt

8 april 1988
der fliegende holländer/conductor horst stein

29 march 1989
der rosenkavalier/conductor horst stein

27 september 1992
fidelio/conductor leopold hager

29 september 1992
ariadne auf naxos/conductor ulf schirmer

25 october 1993
lucia di lammermoor/conductor anton guadagno

26 october 1993
il trovatore/conductor zubin mehta

4 october 1998
götterdämmerung/conductor peter schneider

6 october 1998
mefistofele/conductor fabio luisi

197

23 october 1999
la juive/conductor simone young

25 october 1999
salome/conductor peter schneider

26 october 1999
rienzi/conductor peter schrottner

30 march 2001
palestrina/conductor peter schneider

31 march 2001
lulu/conductor michael boder

1 april 2001
götterdämmerung/conductor simone young

29 may 2003
tristan und isolde/conductor christian thielemann

1 june 2003
andrea chenier/conductor adam fischer

2 june 2003
tristan und isolde/conductor christian thielemann

26 june 2005
parsifal/conductor christian thielemann

23 january 2008
die meistersinger von nürnberg/conductor christian thielemann

25 november 2015
elektra/conductor peter schneider

26 november 2015
hänsel und gretel/conductor christian thielemann

27 november 2015
le nozze di figaro/conductor james gaffigan

Books published by Travis & Emery Music Bookshop:

Anon.: Hymnarium Sarisburiense, cum Rubricis et Notis Musicis.
Anon.: Säcularfeier des Geburtstages von Ludwig van Beethoven
Agricola, Johann Friedrich from Tosi: Anleitung zur Singkunst.
Allen, Percy: The Stage Life of Mrs. Stirling: With ... C19th Theatre
Bach, C.P.E.: edited W. Emery: Nekrolog or Obituary Notice of J.S. Bach.
Bateson, Naomi Judith: Alcock of Salisbury
Bathe, William: A Briefe Introduction to the Skill of Song
Berlioz, Hector: Autobiography of Hector Berlioz, (2 vols.)
Buckley, Robert John: Sir Edward Elgar
Burney, Charles: The Present State of Music in France and Italy
Burney, Charles: The Present State of Music in Germany, The Netherlands ...
Burney, Charles: Account of an Infant Musician
Burney, Charles: An Account of the Musical Performances ... Handel
Burney, Karl: Nachricht von Georg Friedrich Handel's Lebensumstanden.
Burns, Robert: The Caledonian Musical Museum .. Best Scotch Songs. (1810)
Cobbett, W.W.: Cobbett's Cyclopedic Survey of Chamber Music. (2 vols.)
Corrette, Michel: Le Maitre de Clavecin
Cox, John Edmund: Musical Recollections of the Last Half Century. (2 vols.)
Crimp, Bryan: Dear Mr. Rosenthal ... Dear Mr. Gaisberg ...
Crimp, Bryan: Solo: The Biography of Solomon
Crotch, William: Substance of Several Courses of Lectures on Music
d'Indy, Vincent: Beethoven: Biographie Critique
d'Indy, Vincent: Beethoven: A Critical Biography
d'Indy, Vincent: Cesar Franck (in English)
d'Indy, Vincent: César Franck (in French)
Dianna, B.A.: Benjamin Britten's Holy Theatre
Dolge, Alfred: Pianos and Their Makers. A Comprehensive History
Fischhof, Joseph: Versuch einer Geschichte des Clavierbaues. (Faksimile 1853).
Fuller-Maitland, J.A.: The Music of Parry and Stanford
Geminiani, Francesco: The Art of Playing the Violin.
Häuser: Musikalisches Lexikon. 2 vols in one.
Hawkins, John: A General History of the Science & Practice of Music (5 vols.)
Holmes, Edward: A Ramble among the Musicians of Germany
Hopkins, Antony: The Concertgoer's Companion - Bach to Haydn.
Hopkins, Antony: The Concertgoer's Companion – Holst to Webern.
Hopkins, Antony: Music All Around Me
Hopkins, Antony: Sounds of Music / Sounds of the Orchestra
Hopkins, Antony: The Nine Symphonies of Beethoven
Hopkins, Antony: Understanding Music

Books published by Travis & Emery Music Bookshop:

Hopkins, Edward & Rimboult, Edward: The Organ. Its History & Construction.
Hunt, John: - see separate list of discographies at the end of these titles
Iliffe, Frederick: The Forty-Eight Preludes and Fugues of John Sebastian Bach
Isaacs, Lewis: Hänsel and Gretel. A Guide to Humperdinck's Opera.
Isaacs, Lewis: Königskinder (Royal Children). Guide to Humperdinck's Opera.
Kastner: Manuel Général de Musique Militaire
Kenney, Charles Lamb: A Memoir of Michael William Balfe
Klein, Hermann: Thirty years of musical Life in London, 1870-1900
Lacassagne, M. l'Abbé Joseph : Traité Général des élémens du Chant
Lascelles (née Catley), Anne: The Life of Miss Anne Catley.
McCormack, John: John McCormack: His Own Life Story.
Mainwaring, John: Memoirs of the Life of the Late George Frederic Handel
Malcolm, Alexander: A Treaty of Music: Speculative, Practical and Historical
Manshardt, Thomas: Aspects of Cortot
Marx, Adolph Bernhard: Die Kunst des Gesanges, Theoretisch-Practisch
May, Florence: The Life of Brahms
May, Florence: The Girlhood Of Clara Schumann: Clara Wieck And Her Time.
Mellers, Wilfrid: Angels of the Night: Popular Female Singers of Our Time
Mellers, Wilfrid: Bach and the Dance of God
Mellers, Wilfrid: Beethoven and the Voice of God
Mellers, Wilfrid: Caliban Reborn - Renewal in Twentieth Century Music
Mellers, Wilfrid: Darker Shade of Pale, A Backdrop to Bob Dylan
Mellers, Wilfrid: François Couperin and the French Classical Tradition
Mellers, Wilfrid: Harmonious Meeting
Mellers, Wilfrid: Le Jardin Retrouvé, The Music of Frederic Mompou
Mellers, Wilfrid: Music and Society, England and the European Tradition
Mellers, Wilfrid: Music in a New Found Land: … … American Music
Mellers, Wilfrid: Romanticism and the Twentieth Century (from 1800)
Mellers, Wilfrid: The Masks of Orpheus: …… the Story of European Music.
Mellers, Wilfrid: The Sonata Principle (from c. 1750)
Mellers, Wilfrid: Vaughan Williams and the Vision of Albion
Newmarch, Rosa: Henry J. Wood
Newmarch, Rosa: Jean Sibelius
Newmarch, Rosa: Mary Wakefield, a Memoir
Newmarch, Rosa: The Concert-Goer's Library
Newmarch, Rosa: The Music of Czechoslovakia
Newmarch, Rosa: The Russian Opera.
Nicholas, Jeremy: Godowsky, the Pianists' Pianist
Niecks, Frederick: The Life oc Chopin. (2 vols.)

Books published by Travis & Emery Music Bookshop:

Panchianio, Cattuffio: Rutzvanscad Il Giovine
Pearce, Charles: Sims Reeves, Fifty Years of Music in England.
Pepusch, John Christopher: A Treatise on Harmony ...
Pettitt, Stephen: Philharmonia Orchestra: A Record of Achievement, 1948-1985
Pettitt, Stephen (ed. Hunt): Philharmonia Orchestra: Discography 1945-1987
Playford, John: An Introduction to the Skill of Musick.
Porte, John: Sir Charles Villiers Stanford.
Quantz, Johann: Versuch einer Anweisung die Flöte traversiere zu spielen.
Rameau, Jean-Philippe: Code de Musique Pratique, ou Methodes.
Rameau, Jean-Philippe: Erreurs sur La Musique dans l'Encyclopédie
Rastall, Richard: The Notation of Western Music.
Rimbault, Edward: The Pianoforte, Its Origins, Progress, and Construction.
Rousseau, Jean Jacques: Dictionnaire de Musique
Rubinstein, Anton : Guide to the proper use of the Pianoforte Pedals.
Sainsbury, John S.: Dictionary of Musicians. (1825). (2 vols.)
Schumann, Clara & Brahms, Johannes: Letters 1853-1896. (2 vols.)
Scott-Sutherland: Arnold Bax
Serré de Rieux, Jean de : Les dons des Enfans de Latone
Simpson, Christopher: A Compendium of Practical Musick in Five Parts
Smyth, Ethel: Impressions That Remained. (2 vols.)
Spohr, Louis: Autobiography
Spohr, Louis: Grand Violin School
Tans'ur, William: A New Musical Grammar; or The Harmonical Spectator
Terry, Charles Sanford: Bach's Chorals – Parts 1, 2 and 3.
Terry, Charles Sanford: John Christian Bach
Terry, Charles Sanford: J.S. Bach's Original Hymn-Tunes - Congregational Use.
Terry, Charles Sanford: Four-Part Chorals of J.S. Bach. (German & English)
Terry, Charles Sanford: Joh. Seb. Bach, Cantata Texts, Sacred and Secular.
Terry, Charles Sanford: The Origins of the Family of Bach Musicians.
Tosi, Pierfrancesco: Opinioni de' Cantori Antichi, e Moderni
Tosi, Pierfrancesco: Observations on the Florid Song.
Tovey, Donald Francis: A Musician Talks, The Integrity of Music
Tovey, Donald Francis: A Musician Talks, Musical Textures
Tovey, Donald Francis: A Companion to "The Art of the Fugue" J.S. Bach
Tovey, Donald Francis: A Companion to Beethoven's Pianoforte Sonatas
Tovey, Donald Francis: Beethoven
Tovey, Donald Francis: Essays in Musical Analysis. (6 vols.).
Tovey, Donald Francis: The integrity of music
Tovey, Donald Francis: Musical Textures

Books published by Travis & Emery Music Bookshop:

Tovey, Donald Francis: Some English Symphonists
Tovey, Donald Francis: The Main Stream of Music.
Van der Straeten, Edmund: History of the Violoncello, The Viol da Gamba ...
Van der Straeten, Edmund: History of the Violin, Its Ancestors... (2 vols.)
Walther, J. G. [Waltern]: Musicalisches Lexikon [Musikalisches Lexicon]
Wagner, Richard: Beethoven (Leipzig 1870)
Wagner, Richard: Lebens-Bericht (Leipzig 1884)
Wagner, Richard: The Musaic of the Future (Translated by E. Dannreuther).
Wyndham, Henry Saxe: The Annals of Covent Garden Theatre. (2 vols.)
Zwirn, Gerald: Stranded Stories From The Operas

Music published by Travis & Emery Music Bookshop:

Bach, Johann Sebastian: Sacred Songs for SCTB, arranged by Franz Wullner.
Bax, Arnold: Symphony #5, Arranged for Piano Four Hands by Walter Emery
Beranger, Pierre Jean de: Musique Des Chansons de Beranger: Airs Notes ...
Bizet, Georges: Djamileh. Vocal Score.
Donizetti, Gaetano: Betly. Dramma Giocoso in Due Atti. Vocal Score.
Frescobaldi, Girolamo: D'Arie Musicali per Cantarsi. Primo & Secondo Libro.
Handel, Purcell, Boyce, Greene ... Calliope or English Harmony: Volume First.
Hopkins, Antony: Sonatine
Purcell, Henry et al: Harmonia Sacra ... The First Book, (1726)
Purcell, Henry et al: Harmonia Sacra ... Book II (1726)
Sullivan, Arthur Seymour: Ivanhoe. Vocal score.
Sullivan, Arthur Seymour: The Rose of Persia. Vocal Score.
Weckerlin, Jean-Baptiste: Chansons Populaires du Pays de France

Other Books, not on Music:

Anon: A Collection of Testimonies Concerning Several Ministers of the Gospel Amongst People called Quakers, Deceased. [Facsimile of 1760 edn.].
Sandeman-Allen, Arthur: Bee-keeping with Twenty hives.

Available from: Travis & Emery at 17 Cecil Court, London, UK.
(+44) (0) 20 7 240 2129. email on sales@travis-and-emery.com .

Discographies by John Hunt.

3 Italian Conductors and 7 Viennese Sopranos: 10 Discographies: Arturo Toscanini, Guido Cantelli, Carlo Maria Giulini, Elisabeth Schwarzkopf, Irmgard Seefried, Elisabeth Gruemmer, Sena Jurinac, Hilde Gueden, Lisa Della Casa, Rita Streich.

A Gallic Trio: 3 Discographies: Charles Muench, Paul Paray, Pierre Monteux.

A Notable Quartet: 4 Discographies: Gundula Janowitz, Christa Ludwig, Nicolai Gedda, Dietrich Fischer-Dieskau.

American Classics: The Discographies of Leonard Bernstein & Eugene Ormand

Antal Dorati 1906-1988: Discography and Concert Register.

Austro-Hungarian Pianists, Discographies of Lili Kraus, Friedrich Gulda, Ingrid Haebler

Back From The Shadows: 4 Discographies: Willem Mengelberg, Dimitri Mitropoulos, Hermann Abendroth, Eduard Van Beinum.

Carlo Maria Giulini: Discography and Concert Register.

Columbia 33CX Label Discography.

Concert Hall Discography: Concert Hall Society and Concert Hall Record Club

Conductors On The Yellow Label: 8 Discographies: Fritz Lehmann, Ferdinand Leitner, Ferenc Fricsay, Eugen Jochum, Leopold Ludwig, Artur Rother, Franz Konwitschny, Igor Markevitch.

Dirigenten der DDR: Conductors of the German Democratic Republic

From Adam to Webern: the Recordings of von Karajan.

Frosh: Discography of the Richard Strauss Opera Die Frau ohne Schatten

Giants of the Keyboard: 6 Discographies: Wilhelm Kempff, Walter Gieseking, Edwin Fischer, Clara Haskil, Wilhelm Backhaus, Artur Schnabel.

Gramophone Stalwarts: 3 Separate Discographies: Bruno Walter, Erich Leinsdorf, Georg Solti.

Great Violinists: 3 Discographies: David Oistrakh, Wolfgang Schneiderhan, Arthur Grumiaux.

Hans Knappertsbusch: Kna: Concert Register and Discography of Hans Knappertsbusch, 1888-1965. Second Edition.

Her Master's Voice: Concert Register and Discography of Dame Elisabeth Schwarzkopf [Third Edition].

Hungarians in Exile: 3 Discographies: Fritz Reiner, Antal Dorati, George Szell.

Leopold Stokowski (1882-1977): Discography and Concert Register

Leopold Stokowski: Discography and Concert Listing.

Leopold Stokowski: Second Edition of the Discography.

Makers of the Philharmonia: 11 Discographies Alceo Galliera, Walter Susskind, Paul Kletzki, Nicolai Malko, Issay Dobrowen, Lovro Von Matacic, Efrem Kurtz, Otto Ackermann, Anatole Fistoulari, George Weldon, Robert Irving.

Metropolitan Sopranos: 4 Discographies: Rosa Ponselle, Eleanor Steber, Zinka Milanov, Leontyne Price.

Mezzo and Contraltos: 5 Discographies: Janet Baker, Margarete Klose, Kathleen Ferrier, Giulietta Simionato, Elisabeth Hoengen.

Mid-Century Conductors and More Viennese Singers: 10 Discographies: Karl Boehm, Victor De Sabata, Hans Knappertsbusch, Tullio Serafin, Clemens Krauss, Anton Dermota, Leonie Rysanek, Eberhard Waechter, Maria Reining, Erich Kunz.

More 20th Century Conductors: 7 Discographies: Eugen Jochum, Ferenc Fricsay, Carl Schuricht, Felix Weingartner, Josef Krips, Otto Klemperer, Erich Kleiber.

More Giants of the Keyboard: 5 Discographies: Claudio Arrau, Gyorgy Cziffra, Vladimir Horowitz, Dinu Lipatti, Artur Rubinstein.

More Musical Knights: 4 Discographies: Hamilton Harty, Charles Mackerras, Simon Rattle, John Pritchard.

Musical Knights: 6 Discographies: Henry Wood, Thomas Beecham, Adrian Boult, John Barbirolli, Reginald Goodall, Malcolm Sargent.

Philharmonic Autocrat 1: Discography of: Herbert Von Karajan [3rd Edition]

Philharmonic Autocrat 2: Concert Register of Herbert Von Karajan 2nd. Ed.

Philharmonic Autocrat: Discography of Herbert von Karajan (1908-1989). 4th Ed..

Philips Minigroove: Second Extended Version of the European Discography.

Pianists For The Connoisseur: 6 Discographies: Arturo Benedetti Michelangeli, Alfred Cortot, Alexis Weissenberg, Clifford Curzon, Solomon, Elly Ney.

Record Pioneers: Richard Strauss, Hans Pfitzner, Oskar Fried, Oswald Kabasta, Karl Muck, Franz Von Hoesslin, Karl Elmendorff.

Sächsische Staatskapelle Dresden: Complete Discography.

Singers of the Third Reich: 5 Discographies: Helge Roswaenge, Tiana Lemnitz, Franz Voelker, Maria Mueller, Max Lorenz.

Singers on the Yellow Label: 7 Discographies: Maria Stader, Elfriede Troetschel, Annelies Kupper, Wolfgang Windgassen, Ernst Haefliger, Josef Greindl, Kim Borg

Six Wagnerian Sopranos: 6 Discographies: Frieda Leider, Kirsten Flagstad, Astrid Varnay, Martha Moedl, Birgit Nilsson, Gwyneth Jones.

Staatskapelle Berlin. The shellac era 1916-1962.

Sviatoslav Richter: Pianist of the Century: Discography.

Teachers and Pupils: 7 Discographies: Elisabeth Schwarzkopf, Maria Ivoguen, Maria Cebotari, Meta Seinemeyer, Ljuba Welitsch, Rita Streich, Erna Berger

Tenors in a Lyric Tradition: 3 Discographies: Peter Anders, Walther Ludwig, Fritz Wunderlich.

The Art of the Diva: 3 Discographies: Claudia Muzio, Maria Callas, Magda Olivero.

The Furtwaengler Sound Sixth Edition: Discography and Concert Listing.

The Furtwängler Sound. Discography of Wilhelm Furtwängler. Seventh Edition.

The Great Dictators: 3 Discographies: Evgeny Mravinsky, Artur Rodzinski, Sergiu Celibidache.

The Lyric Baritone: 5 Discographies: Hans Reinmar, Gerhard Huesch, Josef Metternich, Hermann Uhde, Eberhard Waechter.

The Post-War German Tradition: 5 Discographies: Rudolf Kempe, Joseph Keilberth, Wolfgang Sawallisch, Rafael Kubelik, Andre Cluytens.

Wagner Im Festspielhaus: Discography of the Bayreuth Festival.

Wiener Philharmoniker 1 - Vienna Philharmonic and Vienna State Opera Orchestras: Discography Part 1 1905-1954.

Wiener Philharmoniker 2 - Vienna Philharmonic and Vienna State Opera Orchestras: Discography Part 2 1954-1989.

Wiener Staatsoper: 348 complete relays

Available from: Travis & Emery at 17 Cecil Court, London, UK.
(+44) (0) 20 7 240 2129. email on sales@travis-and-emery.com .

© Travis & Emery 2016

www.ingramcontent.com/pod-product-compliance
Lightning Source LLC
Chambersburg PA
CBHW071844230426
43671CB00012B/2059